GEMS
Leader's Handbook

Welcome to the GEMS Leadership Team!

Helping you introduce others to the GEMS series is a major interest of the project staff. The purpose of the GEMS Leader's Handbook is to provide you, the GEMS Associate or Leader, with assistance in accomplishing that task.

Every situation and audience is different, and every workshop leader has his or her own style. Consequently, there is no one recipe for success.

In the following pages we present a distillation of our experiences in introducing teachers to GEMS, in the hope you will glean elements useful in your situation.

LHS GEMS

GEMS
Great Explorations in Math and Science
Lawrence Hall of Science
University of California

Acknowledgments

The second and third editions of the *GEMS Leader's Handbook* were revised by Jacqueline Barber, Lincoln Bergman, Kimi Hosoume, Cary Sneider, and Carolyn Willard. The first edition was produced as part of a three-year grant from the National Science Foundation, which included the presentation of GEMS workshops nationwide.

The authors of the first edition were Jacqueline Barber, Lincoln Bergman, and Cary Sneider. The GEMS project would like to thank all those who assisted in reviewing that first version of the GEMS Leader's Handbook, particularly Elizabeth Stage and Carolyn Willard. Earlier input was provided by Katharine Barrett, Jean Echols, Robert C. Knott, and Jennifer White. GEMS Trial Site Directors, including Richard Clark, Richard Golden, Phillip Larsen, Amy Lowen, and Sher Renkin, took part in discussions concerning this document. We have been greatly assisted by different leader's guides and related materials prepared by other curriculum projects at the Lawrence Hall of Science, especially the *SAVI/SELPH Leadership Trainer's Manual* by Linda De Lucchi and Larry Malone.

In addition, hundreds of teachers and educators across the country presented GEMS activities in their classrooms during the testing process; their comments and suggestions contributed immensely to the GEMS series. They are listed in the GEMS guides they played a part in shaping.

GEMS was launched in 1984 thanks to grants from the A.W. Mellon Foundation and the Carnegie Corporation of New York, with equipment donations from Apple Computer. Under a National Science Foundation grant, GEMS Leader's Workshops were held nationally. GEMS has also received and gratefully acknowledges contributions from: the people at Chevron USA; the Hewlett Packard Company; McDonnell-Douglas Employee's Community Fund and Foundation; Employees Community Fund of Boeing California and Boeing Corporation; Join Hands, the Health and Safety Educational Alliance; the Microscopy Society of America (MSA); the Shell Oil Company Foundation; the Crail-Johnson Foundation; and the William K. Holt Foundation This support does not imply responsibility for statements or views expressed in publications of the GEMS program. We welcome your comments, criticisms, and suggestions. Write or call:

LHS GEMS
Lawrence Hall of Science
University of California
Berkeley, CA 94720-1500
(510) 642-7771

On the web at: lawrencehallofscience.org/gems

The GEMS Staff

Principal Investigator
Glenn T. Seaborg

Director
Jacqueline Barber

Associate Director
Kimi Hosoume

Associate Director/Principal Editor
Lincoln Bergman

Science Curriculum Specialist
Cary Sneider

Mathematics Curriculum Specialist
Jaine Kopp

GEMS Network Director
Carolyn Willard

GEMS Workshop Coordinator
Laura Tucker

Staff Development Specialists
Lynn Barakos, Katharine Barrett, Kevin Beals, Ellen Blinderman, Beatrice Boffen, Gigi Dornfest, John Erickson, Stan Fukunaga, Philip Gonsalves, Linda Lipner, Debra Sutter

Distribution Coordinator
Karen Milligan

Workshop Administrator
Terry Cort

Materials Manager
Vivian Tong

Financial Assistant
Alice Olivier

Distribution Representative
Felicia Roston

Shipping Assistants
Ben Arreguy, Bryan Burd

GEMS Marketing and Promotion Director
Gerri Ginsburg

Marketing Representative
Matthew Osborn

Senior Editor
Carl Babcock

Editor
Florence Stone

Principal Publications Coordinator
Kay Fairwell

Art Director
Lisa Haderlie Baker

Designers
Carol Bevilacqua, Rose Craig, Lisa Klofkorn

Staff Assistants
Kasia Bukowinski, Larry Gates, Trina Huynh, Steve Lim, Jim Orosco, Christine Tong

International Standard Book Number: 0-924886-52-8

©1988 The Regents of the University of California

Reprinted with revisions, 1994, 1997, 2000. Permission to reproduce these materials is granted for workshop or classroom use only. For all other purposes, request permission in writing from the GEMS program at the Lawrence Hall of Science.

Contents

What is a GEMS Leader? 5

Goals of the GEMS Program 6

The Making of a GEM 7

Mining and Refining GEMS 8

Successful Workshop Strategies 11

Presenting GEMS in a Variety of Situations 12

    Sample Agenda: 3-Hour GEMS Workshop 13

    Sample Agenda: 5-Hour GEMS Workshop 14

    A Multiple-Day Comprehensive Course 15

Special Concerns of Various Audiences 16

Providing Continuing Support 17

The GEMS National Network 18

Features

    Are GEMS Activities Educationally Effective? 19

    GEMS and Research: Three Case Studies 28

    1001 Ideas to Promote Activity-Based Science 33

Summing Up 77

Leadership and Workshop Support Form 78

Bubble Festival

Group Solutions

Paper Towel Testing

Build It! Festival

Dry Ice Investigations

What is a GEMS Leader?

"I regularly present in-service workshops using GEMS and am familiar with many guides in the series. However, I have never attended an official GEMS Leader's Workshop. Am I a GEMS Leader?"

We receive many inquiries such as this from GEMS-using educators around the nation. The short answer to the question is "YES." A slightly more detailed answer may be helpful to clarify the wide diversity of ways educators become GEMS Leaders.

You should be aware that the circumstances and situations under which "official" GEMS Leaders Workshops have been conducted have been and are diverse. For instance, the first series of GEMS Leader's Workshops, funded by the National Science Foundation, were half-day workshops. While a half-day is not enough to "make" a Leader, we felt justified in offering such a short format because a requirement for attending these workshops was that participants already be leaders in science and mathematics education. Thus, the underlying pedagogy of activity-based science and mathematics instruction, as well as how to play a leadership role in a school or district were already understood and practiced. Our charge in the half-day was to communicate the depth and breadth of the GEMS series, so that GEMS would become a tool in the hands of these effective leaders. We also spent some time in each workshop discussing leadership and gathering participant ideas for the feature "1001 Ideas to Promote Activity-Based Science" on page 33.

In some ways, however, given their length, these NSF-sponsored half-day workshops should have been called GEMS "Orientation Workshops for Leaders." Nonetheless, we consider the folks who attended this type of GEMS Leaders's Workshop to be GEMS Leaders. They are leaders in the field and they are knowledgeable about GEMS. We continue to offer workshops in this format as well as slightly longer workshops, approximately one day in length.

There are also many people who have spent two to twenty days with the GEMS staff, receiving in-depth in-service in many guides, as well as engaging in discussions and activities pertaining to the notions involved in "guided discovery" methods, other aspects of the GEMS philosophy, the nature of science and mathematics, and leadership strategies. Some of the participants of these workshops and teacher institutes may have already been leaders in science and mathematics education, while others may have been excellent teachers or in-service providers but relatively new to science and/or mathematics. We consider the participants of this type of GEMS Leader's experience to be GEMS Leaders, too.

There are now more than 50 GEMS Centers or GEMS Network Sites across the country. As we continue to develop these regional GEMS Centers and Sites, leading GEMS Associates at these locations will also conduct GEMS Orientation and Leader's Workshops, thereby increasing the number and variety of situations and circumstances in which GEMS Leaders are created.

Beginning in 1994, GEMS created a new leadership category: the GEMS Associate. A GEMS leader can become a GEMS Associate by taking a GEMS Associate's Workshop, taught by Lawrence Hall of Science Staff, or by having equivalent LHS-taught workshop experience. Associate's Workshops are held periodically at LHS and selected GEMS sites or centers. Associate's II Workshops have also been launched (see page 79).

While these Associate Workshops always include hands-on activities, they emphasize leadership, workshop presentation skills, and an in-depth familiarity with the approach and philosophy of the GEMS series. One of the most important responsibilities of GEMS Associates is their willingness to be on a recommended referral list to present GEMS workshops in the region.

Please see the GEMS Associate announcement on page 79, and watch future issues of the *GEMS Network News* for announcements of future Associate's workshops.

Finally, as GEMS Leaders use GEMS, they introduce many more teachers to GEMS activities. The introduction may be quite brief, as in after-school orientation sessions, while in other situations GEMS Leaders may conduct in-depth workshops comparable to those offered by GEMS staff. The participants in these latter workshops can be considered to be GEMS Leaders as well. Many GEMS Leaders not only conduct orientation, leadership, and specialized GEMS workshops, they also play a role in regional education and coordination, and have set up materials kits, lending libraries, etc. In a sense, they are operating as informal regional centers and doing a great job getting the word out!

So, there are many ways to become a GEMS Leader. Our GEMS motto of flexibility applies to the definition of a GEMS Leader as well. If you are an avid user of GEMS and share what you know about GEMS with other teachers, then consider yourself a GEMS Leader, and please be aware of how much we appreciate your dedicated work. As always, we very much want to know about your workshops and other efforts. Let us hear from you!

Goals of the GEMS Project

The GEMS Project uses an inquiry-driven, activity-based approach to accomplish the following goals:

- Create independent learners and critical thinkers.

- Increase students' understanding of pivotal science and mathematics concepts.

- Promote mastery of key science and mathematics skills.

- Build positive attitudes toward science and mathematics.

Communicating these goals to GEMS teachers is important because they will carry out this mission when they present GEMS activities to their students.

Importantly, as the GEMS catalog and other documents emphasize: "The experiential nature of activity-based science and mathematics makes it especially effective for reaching ALL students. GEMS can serve, for example, as an outstanding and proven resource for students considered 'at risk' of failure. Doing GEMS activities gives all youngsters a positive experience with science, a sense of their own ability to succeed, thus building student confidence.

"Emphasis on teamwork and cooperative learning, the use of a wide variety of learning formats, and reliance on direct experience rather than textbooks helps make GEMS highly appropriate for use with populations that have been historically underrepresented in science and mathematics pursuits and careers. In GEMS activities students are encouraged to work together to discover more, explore a problem, or solve a mystery, rather than fixating on the so-called right answer, or engaging in negatively competitive behavior. Cooperative learning is one of the most effective strategies for bridging and appreciating differences and diversities of background and culture. It is also one of the most effective ways to prepare all students for the work places of the future."

Teachers can read the GEMS *Teacher's Handbook* and other handbooks for more detailed discussions of the GEMS philosophy and approach, including *The Architecture of Reform* (on how GEMS meets national standards), *Once Upon A GEMS Guide* (on making literature connections) and *Insights and Outcomes,* the GEMS assessment handbook. The assessment handbook includes descriptions of assessments that are already built into GEMS activities, as well as a series of "case studies" of many modes of assessment for GEMS and activity-based science

and mathematics. There is also a concise section on assessment in the GEMS *Teacher's Handbook*.

GEMS Leaders may be interested in a brief video overview of the GEMS series, and a short video on the main educational "threads" in GEMS, both available from the GEMS national office. (See page 78 for these and other ways that the GEMS office can be of assistance to you.)

Spanish translations of GEMS data sheets for many GEMS guides are now available.

Under development are handbooks on other key educational topics, as well as more and more GEMS teacher's guides. Check the current GEMS catalog and *GEMS Network News* for announcements of the availability of these new guides and handbooks.

The Making of a GEM

GEMS is the product of an enormous and skilled team of people: curriculum developers, authors, editors, artists, teachers, and students—not to mention the numerous parents, scout leaders, hardware store clerks, rocketry salespeople, earthworms and other critters who have contributed to GEMS.

Teachers considering a new curriculum often want to know how and by whom it was developed. GEMS is not just a bunch of "neat" but untested ideas, thought up by people in offices. GEMS activities have survived multiple rounds of scrutiny and critical use by a diverse group of teachers with hundreds, in some cases thousands, of children. The "Mining and Refining GEMS" metaphor on pages 8–9 provides a glimpse into the long and careful process by which a "GEM" is created.

GEMS activities begin at the Lawrence Hall of Science (LHS), the public science, curriculum development, and research center at the University of California at Berkeley. LHS has a 25-year tradition of excellence and innovation in science and mathematics education, including the development of a number of pioneering hands-on curricula in wide use nationally and around the world. The activities that are destined to become GEMS have been presented to thousands of eager students who take part in the Hall's extensive public educational efforts, at classes held at the Hall, and as part of the diverse outreach offerings to many regional school districts and national institutes. Over the past 25 years these classes and programs, and the hundreds of dedicated educators who have worked on them in a cooperative and selfless spirit, have indeed produced some real GEMS! This large number of creative and highly effective activities, many of them previously undocumented, provides an always-growing, very rich "mother lode" source for GEMS publications. From these we especially seek those that present key and needed concepts and processes in particularly original and involving ways, whose effectiveness and success have stood the test of time and further foster the insatiable curiosity of young minds.

As the mining metaphor demonstrates graphically, there is many a trial test and refinement between the original activities and the published guide. Among the criteria we evaluate as a team as we bring a GEMS guide to birth are: Can the activities be presented in the school classroom by teachers without special background in math and science, using commonly available materials? What are the logistical challenges involved? What is the "GEM-like" essence of a series of activities, the most central, exciting, and compelling aspects that are also among the most educationally effective? How can the activities be written up and structured to ensure that the "guided discovery" essence remains strongly intact, so students make their own discoveries, and the role of the teacher is to facilitate that process happening in the most beneficial ways?

Mining and Refining GEMS

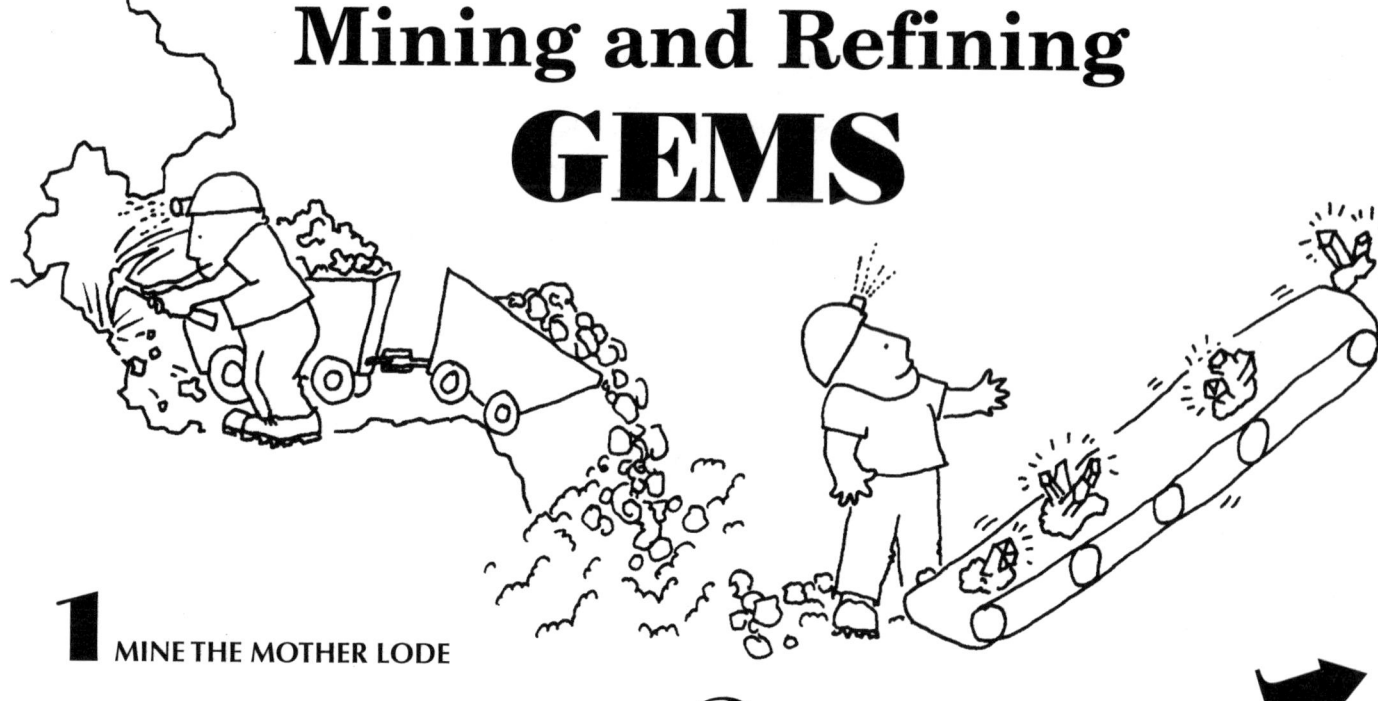

1. MINE THE MOTHER LODE

Classes and activities developed at the Lawrence Hall of Science over the past 25 years are reviewed to identify those that are popular with students and communicate pivotal science and mathematics concepts and processes.

2. SELECT ORE SAMPLES

Reduce the pool of activities by selecting those that:
 a) rely on simple, inexpensive materials;
 b) are likely to work well in typical classroom situations;
 c) require no specialized knowledge to present; and
 d) complement other GEMS units to provide teachers with a full menu of choices.

8. INTRODUCE COMPLETED GEMS NATIONWIDE

Dissemination of completed GEMS units to schools across the nation is in the hands of GEMS Leaders, experienced teachers, and educators who view GEMS guides as useful tools for teaching activity-based science and mathematics in their areas. Leaders conduct workshops for teachers and administrators, provide support for teachers introduced to GEMS materials, and keep in touch with GEMS users nationwide through meetings and the *GEMS Network News*.

7. POLISH AND MOUNT COMPLETED GEMS

GEMS author-developers summarize data from national trials, and complete final revisions of teacher's guides. These are edited, illustrated, and printed in limited quantities, allowing for additional revisions as more teachers in the field begin to use them.

3 CONDUCT THE ACID TEST

GEMS author-developers test potential activities in local classrooms under the close scrutiny of the teacher and another curriculum developer. Activities that do not work well in the classroom are either modified or eliminated.

4 ROUGH CUT GEMSTONES

Revisions suggested by the early classroom tests are incorporated into the first drafts of the GEMS teacher's guides. A committee of experienced curriculum developers and teachers examines and revises the drafts so they are clear and brief, yet contain all details needed to teach the units.

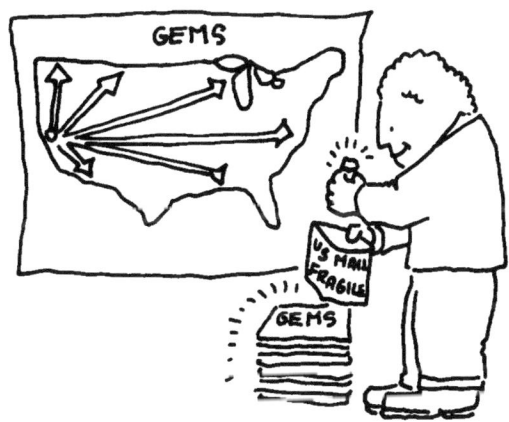

6 FINE CUT FOR WIDE VARIETY OF SETTINGS

Data from local trials are incorporated into revised teacher's guides and sent to 25 teachers at five national trial sites. Site Directors conduct introductory workshops and gather evaluation forms from teachers for all sessions of each unit, and these are sent to GEMS Headquarters at the Lawrence Hall of Science.

5 TRY OUT IN DIFFERENT SETTINGS

Twenty-five local teachers are given guides and invited to teach the units. These local field trials are diverse: urban and rural schools; experienced and novice teachers, and a wide range of age levels. Sessions are observed and recorded by a GEMS team member, and teachers fill out detailed evaluation forms.

The many hundreds of teachers who have helped us during the local and national trial testing process are listed as reviewers at the front of the guides. They play an absolutely crucial role in ensuring that these exciting activities work in the classroom, and that the step-by-step instructions are written clearly. Sometimes an activity that has worked well in the science center setting cannot be successfully adapted to the classroom, for example, perhaps it requires elaborate equipment. At many other times, the combined experience of the GEMS staff and the dedicated teachers who try out the activities comes up with wonderful ways to adapt for the classroom and to improve an activity besides! The detailed feedback of these teachers and the work of their students often spark new and better ways of presentation and great ideas for "Going Furthers." There is always room for improvement and we frequently revise GEMS guides based on additional teacher comment.

Our goal is to make a real and lasting contribution, along with many other talented teachers, educators, and curriculum projects around the country, to science and mathematics education. We share the vision of a more scientifically literate populace, with special attention to the young people of all backgrounds whose ability to think for themselves, work cooperatively to solve problems, and make tough decisions about many controversial and pressing issues, will build the future.

Funding for the development, testing, and production of GEMS guides and for workshops and other dissemination efforts has come from a number of sources, and these are noted in Acknowledgments at the front of this handbook and in other publications. We are extremely grateful for this assistance, and we applaud these funders for their recognition of the deep-going need for bringing activity-based science and mathematics to all students.

An initial series of grants in the mid-1980s, from the A.W. Mellon Foundation and the Carnegie Corporation of New York, enabled the development, testing, and publication of the first GEMS guides. A National Science Foundation grant included presentation of GEMS workshops nationwide and helped establish our growing national network. Grants from the Hewlett Packard Company included workshops and the *Frog Math* and *Mystery Festival* guides. The people at Chevron USA helped sponsor the *Bubble Festival* guide as well as a series of GEMS Leaders workshops. A grant from the McDonnell Douglas Employees Community Fund and Foundation (now Boeing) helped establish the first GEMS Center, which evolved an innovative and effective model that has been applied nationwide. Boeing/McDonnell contributions also enabled the development, testing, and publication of *Group Solutions, Investigating Artifacts, In All Probability, Moons of Jupiter, Terrarium Habitats, Build It! Festival, Sifting Through Science, On Sandy Shores, Math Around the World, Dry Ice Investigations, Messages from Space, Only One Ocean,* and *Ocean Currents*.

A number of GEMS guides, *including Acid Rain* and *Global Warming,* as well as the growing number of guides in the popular GEMS/PEACHES early childhood series, were funded by the GEMS program directly, as are all of the GEMS handbooks and the GEMS Network News newsletter. The GEMS program makes every effort to keep the cost of all of its publications as economical as possible. We are very well aware of the difficult economic conditions for individual teachers and many school systems.

The GEMS program's mission is to encourage the widespread and effective use of high-quality activity-based science and mathematics. As a non-profit educational insitution, our guide prices are determined primarily by the requirement that we have enough funds to revise and reprint guides as the inventory becomes depleted, and to support the staff necessary to ensure a responsive ordering and communications process with GEMS Leaders and Associates and others who are part of our rapidly growing GEMS network. We continue to seek funding for development, testing, and production of new guides, as well as for specialized workshops, GEMS Centers in many regions of the country, and other educational projects.

Successful Workshop Strategies

One general rule applies to all presentations: do hands-on activities, and start them right away. Like children and other people, teachers learn best by doing. This technique of modeling activities enables teachers to appreciate the problems and triumphs their students are likely to encounter, and be ready to teach the very next day.

Most workshop situations will not provide enough time for you to model all of the activities you would like to present. We have found that it is better to present one or two activities thoroughly, and give a brief overview of the rest of the units, rather than allot equal but inadequate time for every activity. On occasion it is expedient to briefly demonstrate an activity or two to expose the audience to the scope and depth of the GEMS series, without taking the time to do the activities completely.

While the most important part of any workshop is doing activities, a dynamic introduction to GEMS will involve a mixture of discussion, activities, and sharing experiences. Timing and variety are very important in maintaining interest. You can alternate activities with discussion about the educational value of those activities. If you have general comments, save them until after the teachers have experienced GEMS for themselves. Allow time for teachers to share their own experiences. Make sure to plan breaks at appropriate times. Teachers like recess too!

A GEMS workshop requires a room with tables and chairs; theatre seating will not do. You will need a table near the front of the room for equipment and demonstrations. An extra table for displaying other GEMS guides provides a nice browsing station. Many activities require water, so locate a nearby source if none is available in the room. A chalkboard is useful.

If you have time to present an overview of the GEMS series, distribute copies of the GEMS *Teacher's Handbook* and have them turn to the GEMS Grade Level Chart at the back of the handbook. GEMS brochures, which include short descriptions of each unit, can also be distributed. Brochures and handbooks can be requested from GEMS headquarters at the Lawrence Hall of Science.

Starting a workshop with an advance organizer that lists the activities to be presented, and gives the overall schedule, helps participants feel comfortable about what is going to happen. If the participants do not already know each other, take a few minutes to have them introduce themselves. Plan a way to conclude so participants feel a sense of resolution. This could be done by having them say what they expect will be most useful to them, what they might need to implement the activities, or if there are other GEMS activities they would be interested in learning about in the future.

Presenting GEMS in a Variety of Situations

GEMS can be the content of a variety of workshops, ranging from a one-hour awareness session to a week-long or even a semester-long comprehensive training workshop. In this section we provide sample agendas for two different workshops and a description of a multi-day intensive course. These might prove useful when you are planning your next presentation. Find the program closest to your requirements, then mold and adapt it to arrive at the presentation that best meets your needs.

Vitamin C Testing

A one- to three-hour introduction to GEMS is the most frequently requested workshop. This is the workshop you use with a school staff, at a convention, or at a one-session invitation to a university methods course. The idea is to make it fast moving and exciting. It's important to touch lightly on all aspects of the program, but devote plenty of time (30-60 minutes at least) to hands-on experiences. One to three hours is enough time to pique teachers' interest in the GEMS series and to provide experience doing one or more GEMS activities.

NOTE: The sample agendas describe three-hour and five-hour presentations. For shorter sessions, cut it off at the amount of time you have and close with materials distribution and an overview of the GEMS series. The time for each hands-on activity can be reduced to 30 minutes, but should not be any shorter than that.

Earth, Moon, and Stars

SAMPLE AGENDA

Three-Hour GEMS Workshop

Time   **Activity and Purpose**

9:00 a.m.   **Introductions**
               Presenter information, participant names, roles, grade levels. Brief overview of the workshop.

9:15   **Oobleck: What Do Scientists Do?**
               Hands-on presentation of Sessions 1 and 2 and an overview of Sessions 3 and 4.
               Experience GEMS activity.
               Introduce GEMS philosophy.

10:30   **Overview of GEMS Series/Video**
               Scope of the GEMS series, anatomy of a guide.

10:45   **Break**
               Browse display set of GEMS guides.

11:00   **Crime Lab Chemistry**
               Hands-on experience with both class sessions.
               Use forensic technique to solve a "mystery."
               Examples of art, literature and language arts connections.

11:50   **Distribution of Materials**
               GEMS Teacher's Handbook, extra brochures, order form for the GEMS Newsletter.

NOON   **End of Workshop**

SAMPLE AGENDA

Five-Hour GEMS Workshop

Time	Activity and Purpose
9:00 a.m.	**Introductions** Presenter information, participant names, roles, grade levels. Brief overview of the workshop.
9:15	**Oobleck: What Do Scientists Do?** Hands-on presentation of Sessions 1 and 2 and an overview of Sessions 3 and 4. *Experience GEMS activity. Introduce GEMS philosophy.*
10:30	**Overview of GEMS Series/Video** *Scope of the GEMS series, anatomy of a guide.*
10:45	**Break** Browse display set of GEMS guides.
11:00	**Fingerprinting** Hands-on presentation of all class sessions in shortened form. *Example of a unit easy for teachers who are new to activity-based lessons. Examples of math, art, literature and language arts connections.*
NOON	**Lunch**
1:00 p.m.	***Bubble-ology*** Presentation of Session 2, "Comparing Bubble Solutions," and brief overview of the whole unit. *Show context and breadth of unit, and experience the science and math in bubble activities.*
2:30	**Overview of Suggested Sequences of GEMS Guides** *Integrate workshop with teachers' needs in planning curriculum.*
3:00	**End of Workshop**

A Multiple-Day Comprehensive Course

Summer in-service programs and preservice courses provide the opportunity for intensive experience using GEMS. Such courses can be short, 12-15 contact hours; a week-long experience of 30-35 hours or longer, or a multiple-session course that extends throughout the academic year—for example, a 3-hour session every two weeks for several months. While a comprehensive course requires a much greater commitment from the GEMS Leader and the participants, the extra effort is well rewarded through a richness of experience that cannot be achieved in any other way.

In multiple-day courses you can design an outline that addresses the needs of the particular group of teachers. While this can be done to some extent in shorter workshops, you will be usually pressed for time just to introduce GEMS in an adequate way. Following are some ideas which might be of use to you in planning a course featuring the GEMS materials.

As you gain experience with several different GEMS units, notice common threads running through the entire series. These threads can help you in planning in-service workshops and methods courses for preservice teachers. We have sometimes organized a course so each day focuses on a different idea.

For example, Day #1 of a four-day course might feature GEMS activities that develop the process of observing, followed by days that focus on the processes of classification, designing controlled experiments, and making inferences. In other situations, we selected the daily topics of guided discovery, questioning, investigation, cooperation, multi-disciplinary teaching, and building students' self confidence and self esteem. Sometimes we chose the daily topics of biology, earth science, chemistry, physics, or applied math. We have organized courses by unifying ideas or themes, such as structure, interactions, and patterns of change. We have also presented sequences of GEMS units whose concepts build from one to the next, such as the triad *Animals in Action*, *Mapping Animal Movements*, and *Mapping Fish Habitats*.

Selecting several activities that demonstrate the idea of the day is a powerful way to enable participants to acquire a depth of understanding about a particular theme, process, subject, or approach. It is sometimes difficult to achieve this when just one example is presented.

If you have time to give teams the responsibility for presenting a GEMS activity to others in the class, do so. This provides an extremely valuable firsthand experience, especially for teachers new to teaching science. A good time to schedule this is near the end of a course, after participants have seen many activities modeled for them and when a certain amount of trust has been built within the group.

It is also valuable to allow time for teachers to create or adapt a science program that they plan to use in their own situations. This works best when several teachers from each school can work together, and when teachers from different schools can hear and borrow from each others' plans.

Don't forget to schedule regular time blocks for teachers to share their knowledge and experiences. While some of this can be done in shorter workshops, it's usually hard to make sufficient time for this. Spend an hour during which participants divulge their favorite sources of inexpensive or free materials. Conduct a brainstorming session on children's literature that builds on GEMS activities. Provide opportunities for teachers to describe other activities that relate to the GEMS units presented. The best resource in a workshop is the teachers themselves.

Special Concerns of Various Audiences

Administrators

When introducing GEMS to superintendents, principals, or curriculum planners, emphasize that the program is designed to be flexible. Administrators will want to know that the introduction of GEMS in their district or school will not disrupt existing curricula or local and state science objectives. A discussion of how GEMS can be used to enrich existing programs and how GEMS units can be sequenced to meet local and state science guidelines is appropriate for this audience.

Principals and superintendents will be interested in knowing that GEMS was developed at the Lawrence Hall of Science, part of the University of California at Berkeley, through years of extensive research and classroom field testing. You might also want to point out the section in the GEMS *Teacher's Handbook* on student evaluation. Be sure to allow time for administrators to participate in an activity or two. In this way, the value of conducting hands-on activities, as well as the need for equipment and preparation time, will speak for itself.

Science Educators and Science Consultants

Science educators and consultants will know science curricula, methods, and approaches. What they will not be familiar with are the specific GEMS units and the scope of the GEMS series. Focus on providing hands-on experiences with as many activities as possible. You may want to allow time for participants to discuss how they might integrate GEMS into their science programs.

Multiple Subject Teachers

Elementary and middle school teachers assigned to teach multiple subjects often do not have much confidence that they can teach science. It's important to get right into hands-on activities and let them experience how non-intimidating they are. Stress science as a motivating medium in which a multitude of interdisciplinary teaching opportunities are possible. Be sure to explain that GEMS guides have everything a teacher needs to present the unit, including details on preparing materials, step-by-step instructions on how to present the activities, and background material for the teacher.

Occasionally you will encounter teachers who are fearful and reluctant to present activity-based science even after they have participated in one or more GEMS activities themselves. Reasons range from feeling that these activities would not work with their particular group of low ability or special education students, to concern about large group sizes and overloaded teaching schedules. In this situation it can be helpful to facilitate a discussion about these issues with teachers who are more experienced in presenting activity-based science and mathematics. These teachers will be able to share their classroom experiences: that students who do poorly in other subjects often excel in activities using manipulatives; that increased focus, enthusiasm, and cooperation from all students during activity times is common; and that teachers derive tremendous rewards from watching students enjoy as they learn.

Parents

Parents can be very enthusiastic proponents of programs for their children. Parent support can be critically important when it comes time to generate funds to set up a program. Parents will want to know that GEMS provides good, solid science, as well as the multitude of other academic and practical experiences their children receive in the process. They'll appreciate oppor-

tunities for their children to exercise curiosity and develop thinking ability. It should not be overlooked that GEMS can help build interests leading to gratifying careers in science and technology. You may want to have the *GEMS Parent's Handbook* on hand, or, even better, consider presenting the parent education workshops in the GEMS *Parent Partners* book.

Preservice Teachers

Those about to embark on a career in the classroom are in the process of building their teaching skills as well as identifying resources they will be able to put into practice in the classroom. It is important to stress the methods used in GEMS activities, and to emphasize the interdisciplinary opportunities provided by a science program such as GEMS. Do lots and lots of activities to imprint preservice teachers with the idea that teaching science and mathematics means interaction with materials and fostering independent thinking.

Education Teams

Sometimes you will be introducing GEMS at a regional meeting or convention. The audience will be self-selecting, so you'll have no control over the number, background, or expertise of the individuals. However, other presentations will be to invited groups. If this is the case, and you will be helping prepare the announcements, you have an opportunity that should not be overlooked. Invite participants from the same school or district to come to the workshop together, in teams of two or three. This starts off dissemination and implementation with internal support at the local site. A team composed of an administrator, a science resource teacher, and a classroom teacher from the same school or district would be ideal. Often we find that communication begun at a GEMS workshop develops into a philosophy of cooperation that spreads throughout other aspects of the curriculum.

Providing Continuing Support

Teachers who are excited about GEMS and wish to present activity-based science to their students need support and encouragement. While experienced teachers may have already established effective support mechanisms, teachers new to activity-based science may be overwhelmed by the logistical details and the student excitement factor.

Teaching teams are a wonderful way to reduce the time, effort, and anxiety that can result from implementing any new educational endeavor, especially activity-based science. There are many effective combinations: new and experienced teachers, math and science teachers, high school and middle school teachers, 2nd and 3rd grade teachers. Teams of teachers can meet to plan cooperative lessons. They can team teach. They can share materials, preparation, and ideas. Most importantly, they can help each other solve problems.

Some school districts have put together a library of GEMS equipment kits that can be checked out by teachers from many different schools. Other districts encourage individual schools to maintain storage areas with kits to be used in that school. Both of these systems work best when one person is assigned to maintain and replenish the equipment kits. Some districts have enlisted the help of a parent organization in filling this role.

Parents can be of assistance as classroom volunteers. Sometimes just having an extra pair of hands can make a world of difference.

Be sure to let teachers know about the *GEMS Network News*, which comes out twice a year and contains articles by and for teachers about how they have used, modified, and adapted GEMS materials. The newsletter can provide a sense of being part of a bigger effort.

The GEMS National Network

The national network of GEMS users can provide support for you! All across the country, teachers are presenting GEMS activities to students, and leaders are introducing teachers to GEMS. Innovations are being developed in the activities themselves. New ways of supporting teachers in presenting hands-on science and mathematics are being implemented. Leaders are finding new avenues to reach teachers who are eager for materials such as these.

A grant from the National Science Foundation enabled our staff to present GEMS workshops to educators nationwide. Write to us for a list of individuals in your region who have attended a GEMS Leader's Workshop. We can also provide you with a list of GEMS trial directors and trial teachers. If you aren't already receiving a copy, write for a subscription to the *GEMS Network News*. Send your ideas, short articles, and anecdotes to the editor of the newsletter so other GEMS teachers and leaders can benefit from your experiences.

On the last page of this handbook is a form that specifies some ways in which the GEMS office can be of assistance to you. The availability of new GEMS publications, as well as other important news, such as the long-awaited production of GEMS materials kits, will be announced in the *GEMS Network News*.

The GEMS network is being strengthened by the establishment of GEMS Centers and GEMS Network Sites is many regions of the country. The response nationwide has been extraordinary! The first GEMS centers, at the Teacher's Center in Huntington Beach, California, has offered a series of intensive GEMS workshops to many teachers from Southern California, through a grant from the McDonnell Douglas Employees Community Fund and Foundation. Similar workshops and a variety of special programs and resources have now been launched at 50 other GEMS Centers and Network Sites. These can range from more modest approaches to large-scale efforts, depending on funding possibilities, as well as on the resources, priorities, and needs of any given region.

As the coordination between the GEMS national office and designated regional centers/sites evolves, and as we continue to seek ways to be of assistance to GEMS Associates and Leaders nationwide, the network will no doubt evolve. Look for detailed reports on the activities of sites and centers in the *GEMS Network News*. If you want to know more about these rapidly growing network activities contact GEMS. If you are interested in possibly establishing such a center or site in your region, please get in touch with Carolyn Willard, GEMS Network Director.

The Educational Effectiveness of GEMS Activities

by Jacqueline Barber, Lincoln Bergman, and Cary Sneider

> For an updated and detailed report on the demonstrated educational effectiveness of GEMS units and related evaluation studies, visit our website at lawrencehallofscience.org/gems and click on "educational effectiveness."

"I've taught GEMS activities to many groups of students, and I can see that they are learning important concepts and developing skills such as observing, experimenting, and critical thinking. But my principal demands proof that the kids learn science from these fun activities. What do research studies say about this?"

While many educators and teachers have long been aware of the powerful impact that "hands-on, minds-on" learning brings, it is certainly useful for administrators, teachers, curriculum developers, and mentor teachers to be reminded of its educational impact and effectiveness.

The following pages are a summary of general research and theory concerning the effectiveness of activity-based science and mathematics. Relevant studies go back more than 20 years. Our summary is not meant to be in any way exhaustive, but simply to provide you, as a GEMS Leader, with some background that you may find useful.

Along with this summary is an article by the GEMS Curriculum Specialist, Cary Sneider, about studies he has conducted on the educational effectiveness of certain GEMS units; including *Earth, Moon, and Stars, Experimenting with Model Rockets, Wizard's Lab*, and several others. We eagerly invite teachers and other educational researchers who have conducted studies on the effectiveness of GEMS materials and activities to write us, so we can continue to update this section of the GEMS *Leader's Handbook* and improve the GEMS program.

A Spectrum of Research Studies

It is important to emphasize that numerous research studies from all over the world have confirmed the general educational effectiveness of the "learning by doing" approach to science and mathematics education, which is at the heart of the "guided discovery" method developed at the Lawrence Hall of Science (LHS) and fully implemented in GEMS activities.

As teachers who do hands-on science or math in the classroom know, the positive effect on student motivation is very strong. Given the typical negative responses to math and science, this enthusiastic transformation in student attitudes is highly important. At the same time, studies show the retention of content, acquisition of skills, and retained comprehension of the processes of science and mathematics is also greatly enhanced through activity-based learning.

One very useful analysis, because it summarizes the results of many studies, is "Laboratory Studies for Elementary School Science" by Ted Bredderman of the State University of New York at Albany, and published in *Science Education* (John Wiley & Sons, Inc., 1985, pages 579–591). In this study, Bredderman analyzes the results of three major curriculum programs that were developed and used in classrooms during the late 1960s and early 1970s. The programs were: the *Elementary Science Study* (ESS), developed at the Educational Development Center, Newton, Massachusetts; *Science—A Process Approach* (SAPA), developed under the direction of the

Commission on Science Education of the American Association for the Advancement of Science; and the *Science Curriculum Improvement Study* (SCIS) developed at the Lawrence Hall of Science (and therefore drawn from the same creative curriculum development approaches that permeate the GEMS guides). By 1977, a national survey found the three programs were being used by 20% of the nation's elementary teachers in grades one through three and 30% of teachers in grades four through six. All the programs were inquiry-based, placed primary emphasis on hands-on laboratory activities, and gave equal attention to the methods and content of science.

Bredderman analyzed the effects of these three national programs on student learning outcomes by quantitatively combining the results of 57 separate studies. Only those studies that included control groups were used. Bredderman found that students enrolled in the new, hands-on programs scored an average of 20 percentile points higher on science process tests than students in conventional programs. His conclusion is worth quoting:

"It appears that the programs designed to encourage the use of laboratory science, starting in the elementary school years, do in fact result in improved student performance in a number of valued curricular areas. . . . How to capitalize on the advantages of the laboratory approach by making it attractive to a wider range of school-based educators remains an unresolved problem for the present reform effort."

Bredderman's bibliography of the 57 studies involved in his analysis would be helpful to those educators or administrators who wish to pursue more information about specific issues or outcomes. Among several articles that relate to the Science Curriculum Improvement Study, for example, are articles by Bowyer and Linn on the effectiveness of SCIS in teaching science literacy; by Linn and Thier on the effects of experimental science on the development of logical thinking in children; and by Lowery, Bowyer, and Padilla on SCIS and student attitudes.

A similar analysis of many controlled studies—by Shymansky, Kyle, and Albert (1983), which appeared in the *Journal of Research in Science Teaching*, pages 387–404, and which synthesized the results of 34 studies of the same three curriculum programs—reached even more positive conclusions. Another study by Kyle compared student results on standardized national science tests. Interestingly, students in Texas who received inquiry-based hands-on instruction in science (the SCIS curriculum) scored as well or better than students taught via textbook and more traditional methods, even when the textbook-based courses focused on content that was to be included on the standardized test, and the inquiry-based instruction did not do so. It is possible that students who take hands-on science do better on achievement tests because the experiential nature of activity-based science and mathematics connects to memory and recall in different ways than a textbook or lecture, thus aiding retention of complex concepts. Kyle is also the co-author of two helpful articles that appeared in *Science and Children* magazine: "What Research Says: Science Through Discovery: Children Love It" (1985) and "What Research Says About Hands-On Science" (1988).

In their excellent summary of research findings—"Hands-On Approaches to Science Teaching: Questions and Answers from the Field and Research" available from the ERIC Clearinghouse for Science, Mathematics, and Environmental Education—Haury and Rillero summarize the conclusions from a variety of research studies about hands-on learning as follows:

- **Hands-on learning has been shown to increase learning and achievement in science content.**
  (Mattheis and Nakayama, 1988;
  Brooks, 1988;
  Saunders and Shepardson, 1984;
  Bredderman, 1982)

- **Research indicates that activity-based science can improve students' attitudes toward science.**
  (Rowland, 1990;
  Kyle, et al., 1985,1988;
  Jaus, 1977)

- **Evidence clearly indicates that hands-on activities increase skill proficiency in processes of science, especially laboratory skills and specific science process skills, such as graphing and interpreting data.**
  (Mattheis and Nakayama, 1988)

- **For both process skills and science content, academically or economically disadvantaged students gained the most from activity-based programs.**
  (Bredderman, 1982)

- **Hands-on learning has been shown to help in the development of language and reading, including reading readiness and oral communications skills.**
  (Bredderman, 1982;
  Quinn and Kessler, 1976;
  Morgan et al., 1977;
  Willman, 1978;
  Huff, 1971;
  Barufaldi and Swift, 1977)

- **Activity-centered classrooms encourage student creativity in problem solving, promote student independence, and help students overcome initial handicaps.**
  (Shymansky and Penick, 1981)

Convergence on a Theory of Learning

The National Center for Science Education (which is a partnership between the Biological Sciences Curriculum Study in Colorado Springs and The NETWORK in Washington, D.C., and Andover, Massachusetts) publishes a number of excellent reports about science education. In "Science and Technology Education for the Middle Years: Frameworks for Curriculum and Instruction" they first note that for much of this century, curriculum materials and educational practices have seen learning as consisting of receiving information dispensed by a teacher or textbook, with the student in a largely passive role. They cite studies showing that such practices "fail to meet the learning needs and requirements of a population that has diverse learning styles and varied ability to conceptualize."

In contrast, the view of learning that has emerged in the last decade, sometimes called **constructivism**, proposes that students, rather than being mostly passive recipients of information, are "active learners who constantly reconstruct their world view, as they try to reconcile past experiences and extant conceptual understanding with new experiences and information."

The report continues: "If the new information is consistent with a learner's existing conceptual framework, the learner can easily assimilate the new knowledge. However, if the new experience and information is sufficiently discrepant from the learner's conceptual framework, then the learner must accommodate that new information by actively constructing his or her framework."

Understood in this way, the prior knowledge of students becomes a crucial factor in learning. Studies have found, for example, that meaningful learning can occur when teachers present new ideas in familiar contexts. But if teachers do not help students relate new information to ideas that the students already hold, they will resort to memorization and superficial learning, which is soon forgotten.

Other research demonstrates that students often have understandings of science that are not congruent with the ideas held by scientists. Several studies indicate that students can cling to these erroneous viewpoints into adulthood. The questions are: How can teachers help students develop more accurate, sophisticated views of concepts to replace their previous misconceptions? How can we help them to construct new meanings that are consistent with those of scientists, and that will transfer to new situations?

Implications for the Best Methods of Teaching

Asking questions

Experienced teachers generally begin a new unit of study by asking questions, to find out their students' ideas about the subject they are about to study. The constructivist theory of education helps us to explain *why* this is an important teaching strategy. GEMS guides use this approach, and suggest questions that teachers might use to start off the unit to find out what their students think. A few build an entire class session around students' initial ideas. For example, "Pick Your Brain about Acid Rain" and a parallel session in the *Global Warming and the Greenhouse Effect* guide, ask students to brainstorm all the things they've heard about acid rain and global warming. Activities such as these give teachers solid information about their students preconceptions, misconceptions, knowledge and lack thereof. They assist the teacher in knowing what to emphasize, and in building the rest of the activities on a solid and appropriate foundation. These "what we think we know" sessions are also very involving activities in themselves, and provide the students with their own framework to compare what they knew when they began a unit with what they've learned during the the unit.

Doing Activities

After finding out the students' ideas in the new area, all GEMS guides urge the teacher to involve their students in active investigations almost immediately. The highly influential *Science for All Americans* by Rutherford and Ahlgren, published in 1990 by the American Association for the Advancement of Science, notes, "Young people can learn most readily about things that are tangible and directly accessible to their senses . . . With experience, they grow in their ability to understand abstract concepts, manipulate symbols, reason logically, and generalize . . ." The National Science Board cites research findings showing that "students are likely to begin to understand the natural world if they work directly with natural phenomena, using their senses to observe and using instruments to extend the power of their senses . . ." This statement is, of course, supported by the rich variety of research findings reported above. Consequently, hands-on activities are the heart of all GEMS units.

Classroom Discussion

According to the constructivist theory, although it is essential that students engage in hands-on activities with real objects and experiments, it is not enough. Students also have to talk about what they have done, the questions their activities raise, and how the activities relate to their earlier ideas. An *Ed Talk* report notes, "Usually, active learning is part of a broader strategy to build students' self-direction using the processes of inquiry, exploration, and experimentation that scientists employ in the real world . . . for the activity to be effective, teachers must link it with specific science concepts and allow ample time for analysis, interpretation, and classroom discussion . . . discussion is essential in a student-centered learning environment. Learning often occurs when students are pressed to explain their ideas in ways that their peers will understand and to defend their viewpoints . . . questioning and discussion have the added bonus of strengthening students' oral communications skills." This emphasis on the other steps of "active learning," in addition to the hands-on activities, aligns with the most current thinking on the ways people learn.

Cooperative Learning

The best way to involve students in productive discussions is through cooperative learning activities. In *all* GEMS activities, students are encouraged to work together to discover patterns, explore a problem, or solve a mystery, rather than fixating on the so-called right answer, or engaging in negatively competitive behavior. In some of the guides, explicit cooperation skills are developed through the activities. For example, in the compelling GEMS guide *Group Solutions*, four students work together in order to solve the problems, games, and puzzles. If just one student

does not participate, it is impossible for the group to find a solution. As stated by Karen Ostlund (1992), "If we expect students to work together, we must teach them social skills just as purposefully and precisely as we teach them academic skills."

Cooperative learning not only helps students to compare and contrast their understanding with others, but also helps to ensure gender equity and access for all students, regardless of racial or ethnic background. The use of a wide variety of learning formats, and reliance on direct experience rather than textbooks, makes GEMS highly appropriate for use with populations that have been historically underrepresented in science and mathematics careers. In fact, cooperative (or collaborative) learning is one of the most effective strategies for bridging and appreciating differences and diversities of background and culture.

Cooperative learning is also one of the most effective ways to prepare students for the workplaces of the future. Many large corporations have contributed generously to innovative science and mathematics education efforts. For one thing, they are concerned that the graduates who apply for jobs with their firms have a good grasp of science, math, and technology. At the same time, many corporate representatives have made it clear to the GEMS staff that the ability of people to work together cooperatively with others is of very great value to them, and in fact may be the single most important attribute in evaluating prospective employees.

Real World Applications

Expressing initial ideas about a new topic, then proceeding to hands-on investigations, followed by discussions in cooperative groups are all clearly important. But they are still not enough. In order for students to learn concepts and to acquire skills that will be useful in new situations, they must have some practice applying them in the real world. A connection to the real world provides a direct relevance that is often appallingly absent in more traditional textbook approaches.

The GEMS environmental guides explore the intersection between science and society, and give students a sense of their own responsibilities and participation in the global future. In many other guides, the real-world connection may be through technology—such as the design of a spacecraft that could land on an ocean of "Oobleck," the design and construction of model rockets, or the creation of settlements on Jupiter's moons. The entire *Oobleck* guide makes a marvelous real-world connection to the work that scientists and engineers actually do. The *Crime Lab Chemistry*, *Fingerprinting*, and *Mystery Festival* guides connect directly to forensic science while helping students recognize the similarities and differences between scientific investigation and solving a mystery. The "Rain Drops, Oil Drops" activity in the *Liquid Explorations* guide was used in schools throughout Alaska to introduce young elementary students to issues raised by a major oil spill.

Still other guides introduce consumer science—as when students evaluate different brands of paper towels, determine the amount of Vitamin C in various juice drinks, or compare bubble-making solutions. *In All Probability* provides direct experience with topics in probability and statistics that raise many societal issues, from diverse careers that involve these areas of mathematics, to state lotteries and advertising claims. *Build It! Festival* connects directly to architecture, construction, and to many other practical applications of mathematics, geometry, and spatial visualization.

On the most direct level, there is a great deal of real-world connection in GEMS activities. On a more global level, the observation skills, scientific and mathematical processes, independent discoveries and investigations, group dynamics, communication skills, controlled experimentation, logical thinking and problem-solving that permeate the GEMS materials are all designed to help prepare students for their real-life roles as active citizens and decision-makers.

Reflections on the Learning Cycle

If we look at the teaching methods discussed above, we see more than a laundry list of ideas. We see the evolution of a set of ideas which formed the underpinnings of the SCIS program. In a seminal paper by Robert Karplus from LHS, and Michael Atkin, now a professor at Stanford University, the concept of the learning cycle was first put forward (1962). The fundamental idea was to structure learning activities so that students would begin with open-ended exploration of real phenomena, and with discussion about their discoveries, ideas, and questions that arose from this initial exploration phase. With the students' interest and attention fully focused, the teacher could now introduce certain concepts or methods to help students solve some of the problems they encounter and construct new meanings. Armed with the new ideas provided by the teacher, the students were then introduced to new activities where they could apply their new knowledge and practice newly acquired skills. Eventually, the students' activities would lead to new discoveries and puzzles, followed by further discussion, introduction of new concepts, and more application. And so, the cycle of exploration, concept introduction, and application would continue.

Over the years, others have proposed variations on the original three-phase learning cycle. The National Center for Improving Science Education suggests a teaching-learning model which, the center states, reflects the approach taken by professionals in science and technology when they learn and apply new skills and information within their fields.

This model assumes as the first stage an "Invitation" as the beginning of a learning process, perhaps in the form of a question or problem for the students to solve, or an observation or demonstration. Invitations can include initial student interactions with hands-on materials. If the question or problem does not engage the learners' interests, then further engagement is unlikely and it is probable that only rote learning will result.

The second stage, "Exploration, Discovery, Creativity," is characterized first by constructive play or informal investigation in which students might try one approach with the materials involved, share their findings with each other, and try other experiments. Depending on past experience and age level, such experiments can become more structured and controlled. Students experiment, observe, record, and interpret data as they solve problems. Students work in cooperative groups, share materials, assist each other, report findings, and begin to link their new findings to modify their concepts.

In the third stage, "Proposing Explanations and Solutions," students and teachers together question, hypothesize, analyze data, build models, clarify concepts, and apply their new knowledge in other contexts. The students and teacher may decide to conduct additional investigations or experiments to help refine the newly developed concepts, resolve differences, and construct a new view of the concept based on what they have learned.

For the fourth stage, "Taking Action," the National Center for Improving Science Education, states, "Once the students have constructed a new view of a concept, they are usually ready to act on that new level of understanding." They might defend a point of view before the class, write a letter to a local authority, raise new questions that call for further investigations, or in other ways take action to demonstrate that they have truly integrated the newly discovered information and concepts into their existing framework of understanding. Also, during this stage, the teacher can assess each student's new level of understanding and the effectiveness of the unit.

Thanks to research on the effectiveness of hands-on science activities, and the theory of constructivism, the learning cycle concept has continued to evolve. We now know how important it is to insert questions at the very beginning of the cycle, to find out the ideas that students have as they begin. The development of cooperative learning techniques has made it possible

to expand and enrich teamwork throughout the cycle. Recent discoveries about global environmental change have given new meaning to and opportunities for the application phase of the learning cycle. And a great many new ideas have come forward about what students can do to feel empowered as active world citizens. The fundamental concept of the learning cycle remains valid, and teachers will find it in many different forms throughout the GEMS series.

National Standards and Assessment

Reforms in science education are sweeping the country. Many states have implemented new science frameworks. Project 2061 of the American Association for the Advancement of Science, the National Science Teachers' Association Scope and Sequence Project, and the National Academy of Science's Standards in Science Education project are all redefining what students should know and how they should learn. These reforms are all based in the constructivist theory of learning. They all recommend hands-on, minds-on teaching methods. They are all supportive of the integration of science content and processes in programs such as GEMS.

Additionally, new methods for assessing student performance are being developed that are appropriate for the hands-on, inquiry-based approaches. At its best, assessment is a highly valuable component of any educational effort, to help determine whether or not the effort is effective and appropriate. It is helpful for teachers, evaluators, and administrators to be aware that many GEMS guides contain "built-in" assessments, in the sense that portions of the activities and/or some of the suggested "going further" activities can be used as highly effective assessment instruments. The assessments are thus embedded in the activities themselves, and as such have been well tested for classroom applicability via the GEMS testing process. The GEMS assessment handbook suggests assessment approaches for all of the GEMS guides, discusses what is meant by authentic assessment, comments on scoring and evaluation, and features a number of "case studies" of excellent and quite diverse types of assessments related to the GEMS series. These "case studies" are classroom tested to ensure that they too are effective, practical, and suitable instruments to assess the concepts, skills, understandings, or attitudes they are intended to assess.

GEMS staff members and many others from the Lawrence Hall of Science and the University of California at Berkeley continue to play important roles on various state, national, and international commissions and conferences to help define the new standards, new methods of assessment, and other educational issues of the future.

GEMS Works

While GEMS is consistent with modern learning theory and widely accepted methods of science teaching, the GEMS activities are not created on the basis of theory alone—far from it. The extensive GEMS classroom testing process is a dynamic mechanism for ensuring quality and clarity. GEMS guides are only published after this intensive and thorough process, including diverse national tests. This testing process includes careful attention to teacher/student input on to a wide range of issues, such as effective communication of the scientific and mathematical content, accessibility of materials, classroom logistics, level of student interest and enthusiasm, and much more. As GEMS Director Jacqueline Barber notes, the GEMS testing process is a powerful partnership between curriculum developers/ teachers at the Lawrence Hall of Science and teachers nationwide.

Each series of activities has led to its own discoveries during the testing process. Feedback is carefully analyzed. Many of the most appealing and imaginative notes and sidebars in the text come from this vast wealth of teacher and student experience and criticism. GEMS activities work in the classroom because they were hammered out in the classroom. They

appeal to teachers because they were shaped by teachers. This process of curriculum development, based on the strong collaboration between teachers and university curriculum developers, helps explain why, when teachers pick up one of these guides, they recognize almost immediately and invariably that the guide speaks their language and will "work."

GEMS is a living, growing, evolving series. We have endeavored to bring high-quality, practical, and effective activity-based science and mathematics activities into classrooms nationwide. We remain open to new educational developments and seek to foster the maximum flexibility for teachers with unique needs and emphases. In addition to our central component of original science and mathematics activities, we place great attention on making connections across the curriculum; combining writing, literature, and the language arts with math and science; helping students actively explore the intersections between science and society; gain deeper understandings of the environmental crisis; and, in general, dedicating our efforts to encouraging the scientific literacy, ability to work constructively together, and independent thinking skills of **all** students.

References

Atkin, J.M. and Karplus, R., "Discovery or Invention?" *The Science Teacher,* Vol. 25, No. 5 (1962): 7–9.

Bredderman, T. "Laboratory Programs for Elementary School Science: A Meta-Analysis of Effects on Learning." *Science Education,* Vol. 69, No. 4 (1985): 579-591.

Bredderman, T. "What Research Says: Activity Science—The Evidence Shows It Matters." *Science and Children,* Vol. 20, No. 1 (1982): 39–41.

Bybee, R.W. et al. *Science and Technology Education for the Elementary Years: Frameworks for Curriculum and Instruction,* The National Center for Improving Science Education (NCISE), Washington, D.C., 1989.

Bybee, R.W. et al. *Science and Technology Education for the Middle Years: Frameworks for Curriculum and Instruction,* (NCISE), Washington, D.C., 1990.

Brooks, R.C. *Improving Student Achievement in Grades 4–6 through Hands-On Materials and Concept Verbalization,* ERIC Document Reproduction Service, No. ED 317 430, Columbus, Ohio 1988.

Haury, E.L. and Rillero, P. *Hands-On Approaches to Science Teaching: Questions and Answers from the Field and Research,* ERIC Clearinghouse, Columbus, Ohio, 1992.

Barufaldi, J.P. and Swift, J.W. "Children Learning to Read Should Experience Science." *The Reading Teacher,* Vol. 30 (1977): 388–393.

Huff, P.E. *The Effects of the Use of Activities of Science: A Process Approach to Oral Communications Skills of Disadvantaged Kindergarten Children.* Ph.D. Dissertation, Ohio State University.

Jaus, H.H. "Activity-Oriented Science. Is It Really That Good?" *Science and Children*, Vol. 14, No. 7 (1977): 26–27.

Kyle, W.C. "Process Science and Standardized Testing: Are They Compatible?" Paper presented at the Annual Meeting of the National Association for Research in Science Teaching, San Francisco, California, March 1989.

Kyle, W.C., Bonnstetter, R.J., Gadsen T. Jr., Shymansky, J.A. "What Research Says About Hands-on Science." *Science and Children*, Vol. 25, No. 7 (1088): 39–40.

Kyle, W.C., Bonnstetter, R.J., McCloskey, J., Fults, B.A. "What Research Says: Science Through Discovery: Students Love It." *Science and Children*, Vol. 23, No. 2 (1985): 39–41.

Loucks-Horsley, S. et al. *Developing and Supporting Teachers for Elementary School Science Education*, The National Center for Improving Science Education, Columbus, Ohio, 1989.

Knapp, M. S., Stearns, M.S., St. John, M., Zucker, A. *Opportunities for Strategic Investment in K–12 Science Education: Options for the National Science Foundation*. National Science Foundationington, D.C. Volume 1, Volume 2, and Summary Report, May/June 1987.

Kober, Nancy *Ed Talk: What We Know About Science Teaching and Learning*, Council for Educational Development and Research, Washington, D.C.

Mattheis, F.E. and Nakayama, G. *Effects of a Laboratory-Centered Inquiry Program on Laboratory Skills, Science Process Skills, and Understanding of Science in Middle Grades Students*, ERIC Document Reproduction Service, No. ED 3-1 148. Columbus, Ohio, 1988.

Morgan, A., et al. "Sciencing Activities as Contributors to the Development of Reading Skills in First Grade Students." *Science Education*, Vol. 61, No. 2 (1977): 135–144.

Ostlund, K.L. "Sizing Up Social Skills." *Science Scope*, Vol. 15, No. 6 (1992): 31–33.

Quinn, M.E. and Kessler, C. *The Relationship Between Science Education and Language Development*. Paper presented at the Annual Meeting of the American Educational Research Association, San Francisco, California, ERIC Document Reproduction Service, No. ED 123 112. Columbus, Ohio, 1976.

Rutherford, F.J. and Ahlgren, A. *Science for All Americans*, Oxford University Press, New York, 1990.

Rowland, P. M. "Using Science Activities to Internalize Locus of Control and Influence Attitudes Toward Science." Paper presented at the Annual Meeting of the National Association for Research in Science Teaching, Atlanta, Georgia, ERIC Document Reproduction Service, No. ED 244 797. Columbus, Ohio, 1990.

Saunders, W.L. and Shepardson, D. *A Comparison of Concrete and Formal Science Instruction upon Science Achievement and Reasoning Ability of Sixth Grade Students*. Paper presented at the Annual Meeting of the National Association for Research in Science Teaching, New Orleans, Louisiana, ERIC Document Reproduction Service, No. ED 244 797. Columbus, Ohio, 1984.

Shymansky, J.A. and Penick, J.E. "Teacher Behavior Does Make a Difference in Hands-On Science Classrooms." *School Science and Mathematics*, Vol. 81, No. 5 (1981): 412–422.

Shymansky, J.A., Kyle, W.C., Alport, J.M. "The effects of new science curricula on student performance." *Journal of Research in Science Teaching*, Vol. 20 (1983): 387–404.

Willman, S. "Science: A Basic for Language and Reading Development," In *What Research Says to the Science Teacher, Volume 1*, National Association of Teachers, Washington, D.C., 1978.

GEMS and Research: Three Case Studies

by Cary Sneider

The studies described below demonstrate three different ways GEMS Curriculum Specialist Cary Sneider used research to enhance the educational effectiveness of GEMS activities.

- *The first is a rigorous study showing that the challenges of controlled experimentation can be successfully presented to students much younger than previously thought.*

- *The second illustrates how GEMS activities can help students gradually come to understand and use powerful concepts that are otherwise very difficult for many students to grasp.*

- *The third demonstrates how attitudes, concepts, and skills can be brought together through tabletop exhibits that form the heart of the GEMS festival guides.*

We invite educational researchers and teachers who have conducted research studies, or developed ideas in teaching and learning that may contribute to the educational effectiveness of GEMS, to send us a copy of your work or write a letter to the GEMS Network News summarizing your findings. We'd love to hear from you!

1 Learning to Control Variables with Model Rockets

When I started teaching at the Lawrence Hall of Science (LHS), I came to understand the importance of involving students in conducting their own investigations. At that time I was a student at U.C. Berkeley's School of Education, where I studied the work of Jean Piaget, the developmental psychologist. Piaget claimed that high school was about the time when students became capable of learning how to design experiments by controlling variables. Recalling the high motivation of model rocketry, which I had taught to high school classes earlier in my teaching career, I decided to devise a model rocketry class to teach students how to design their own controlled experiments. Their challenge would be to conduct experiments in order to find out how to design rockets that would fly higher. Their experiments consisted of pairs of rockets that were different in only one way—such as the shape of the fin or the length of the body tube. All other variables were kept constant.

Judging from student interest and high-level discussions about the experiments, the class was very successful. The high school students designed some wonderfully creative experiments! At the same time, we began to have many opportunities to teach the model rocketry class to students as young as 9 years old. Surprisingly, they did quite well at designing and criticizing controlled experiments—even though Piaget claimed that this was a "formal operational level" skill that could not be learned by children younger than 15 or 16 years old. Surely, this was a mystery worthy of further study!

We worked on the project for about five years. By 1982, and with the help of a National Science Foundation grant, we had conducted a series of studies with students in all sorts of learning situations, including schools, scout organizations, and summer camps. We conducted a one-day workshop for teachers and other youth leaders in how to present the class. Then we conducted both individual interviews and paper-and-pencil questionnaires both before and after students took the class from their newly trained teachers. The elaborate experimental design showed that **children from 9 to 15 years old could significantly improve in their abilities to design and critique controlled experiments as a result of the model rocketry course.**

An important insight resulted from one study at a summer camp that included both boys and girls. As in the other studies, all students who took the model rocketry course improved in their abilities to control experiments. But, the control group of girls who did *not* take model rocketry improved too! The control group of boys, on the other hand, did not. The best explanation seemed to be that the girls talked about their experiments with the other girls, who anticipated taking the class during the next week of camp. There seemed to be a learning effect from talking about controlled experimentation!

An article about these findings was published in 1984 in the journal *Science Education*. The article included an analysis of some 40 studies showing that positive results could be obtained in a wide variety of settings where students were given opportunities to perform controlled experiments. This research has helped guide the development of many GEMS activities. For example, the following three GEMS units (in addition to *Experimenting with Model Rockets*) help students learn controlled experimentation one step at a time:

- In *Hot Water and Warm Homes from Sunlight*, students are introduced to the concept of controlled experimentation through an activity sheet in which they reason about some plants that were given different amounts of fertilizer. They perform experiments that have been designed for them, discuss why it is important to keep all of the possible variables constant, and can go on to design their own experiments.

- In *Bubble-ology*, students are introduced to a technique for measuring the size of bubbles so they can determine which of three soap solutions is best. But they need to think of how to conduct the tests so that all variables are controlled except for the kind of soap solution.

- In *Paper Towel Testing*, students are challenged to design their own experiments to determine which brand of paper towel has greater wet strength, and which is more absorbent. Thus, they must identify the variables and invent experiments that will control them.

The research studies described above provide clear and compelling evidence that such GEMS activities help students understand the concept of a controlled experiment, and improve their abilities to design, conduct, and criticize controlled experiments. Acquiring this key skill is important because it improves students' understanding of what scientists do, and equips them with an important ability for living and working in the modern world.

2 Learning About the Earth's Shape and Gravity

Some years ago I attended a symposium presented by an Israeli educator whose research showed that when students said the Earth is "round," they had some very strange conceptions about what that actually meant. For example, some thought that the Earth is round like a pancake, and Columbus sailed around it as he would around an island. Others thought that the round Earth is a round planet where only astronauts go; or that the Earth we live on is indeed round like a ball, but that we live "on the flat part in the middle."

Shortly after I attended the symposium, I was teaching astronomy in a teacher education program and I presented these results to the teachers. They indignantly doubted that their students might have such bizarre notions. I invited them to participate with me in a research project to determine if students in the San Francisco Bay Area shared these notions as well. Although many were interested, only three of the teachers participated in the entire study, which required the better part of a year. We not only confirmed the results of earlier studies, but we extended them, showing that two separate but related concepts were involved: the Earth's spherical shape *and* the concept of gravity. Our final paper, in the journal *Science Education*, included an analysis of studies from four countries, involving over 600 students, showing that misconceptions about these fundamental concepts were widespread and did not vary significantly from country to country. Furthermore, these misconceptions were only partially overcome by junior high school and some, especially those related to gravity, persisted into high school.

The GEMS unit *Earth, Moon, and Stars* is based on the findings of this research study concerning children's ideas and misconceptions about the Earth's spherical shape and the force of gravity. The GEMS guide starts off from the widely accepted premise that students can overcome such misconceptions by having the opportunity to contrast their own views with the opinions, arguments, and evidence presented by others.

In the first activity, students are asked to imagine that they lived a long time ago, when people thought that the Earth was flat. How might they explain the observation that the Sun went from the west, where it set every night, to the east, where it rose each morning? In this activity, students come up with some very creative flat-Earth models to explain this observation. In many cases, they are able to express their actual misconceptions, and to compare their ideas with others.

In the second activity, students are introduced to the spherical Earth concept. This concept explains the daily motion of the sun as a consequence of the Earth's spinning on its axis once a day. But just as it did for the ancient Greek philosophers who first proposed it, the new model raised new questions, such as: Why don't people fall off the "bottom" of the Earth? Are there really people who live "down there beneath our feet?" The students struggle with these questions, which were developed in the context of the research study described above. The students enjoy arguing and debating the answers to these questions, and the GEMS teacher's guide prepares the teachers to both facilitate the students' discussions, and to present how Aristotle and Newton would answer them. While it is not expected that all students will immediately embrace the modern Newtonian viewpoint, this activity is intended to move students toward a more adequate understanding of the Earth's shape and gravity, and to give them an experience in one aspect of the nature of science —using a model to explain what they see in the sky. Teachers are encouraged to use the questionnaire provided in the guide as a pretest and post-test to assess the degree to which their students have comprehended modern scientific concepts about the Earth's shape and gravity.

Other activities in the *Earth, Moon, and Stars* guide involve students in observing phases of the moon for a month, and using a model made with a lamp to represent the sun, and "moon ball" for each student, to recreate and observe the moon's phases in a concrete situation. The guide explains to the teacher how these observations support and extend the previous activities at two levels. First, the ball-shaped moon serves as another way of thinking about the ball-shaped Earth and how it would appear from space. And secondly, it provides another example of how we can use models to explain observable phenomena. Finally, activities in which students observe how stars appear to move give students insight into how Copernicus inferred the motions of the Earth.

In summary, *Earth, Moon, and Stars* is based on educational research showing that students have many misconceptions about the planet where we

all live. It is also based on the learning theory called "constructivism," which postulates that students will advance in their understanding only if they can recognize the shortcomings of their current points of view, and move towards a more scientific view of the universe.

Other guides in the GEMS series are also designed to teach concepts that research studies have shown to be difficult for students. For example, students learn about density in *Discovering Density*, about triangulation in *Height-O-Meters*, and about convection in *Convection: A Current Event*. We have not had the resources to conduct experimental studies of all GEMS units. However, we have asked all teachers conducting trials of the activities to tell us if they believe their students grasp the essential concepts of the unit. Trial activities become GEMS units only if a national sample of teachers at the recommended grade levels have determined that their students not only enjoy the activities, but also grasp the fundamental concepts.

3. The Wizard's Lab

A few years ago, a researcher from the University of Helsinki in Finland, Matti Erätuuli, came to Lawrence Hall of Science for a sabbatical visit. He collaborated with me to evaluate the educational effectiveness of The Wizard's Lab, which is a physics discovery room that has been under my direction since 1982. Some of the tabletop exhibits in The Wizard's Lab are described in a GEMS guide of the same name. I had run across an article critical of such popular "science playgrounds," and thought it was about time for research to either confirm or deny claims of educational effectiveness.

The Wizard's Lab discovery room contains about 50 tabletop exhibits accompanied by cartoon instructions. (Our observations of other exhibits several years before had indicated that nearly all visitors will pay attention to cartoon instructions, but very few will read a block of text which says the same thing.) We developed an observation instrument—a set of questions and ratings to be used by a trained observer—that enabled us to determine whether or not visitors read the cartoons, whether they used the lab equipment as intended, and whether or not they read the more extensive information available at each exhibit. We noted how they worked with other visitors and whether or not they seemed to be enjoying themselves. The reliability of the observation instrument turned out to be quite high, even though it called for subjective judgments. We analyzed the data statistically to determine the manners in which visitors used the exhibits, and the factors most closely related to appropriate use of the equipment and enjoyment.

We were pleased to find that most visitors either read the cartoon instructions, or had another visitor (usually a parent) read the instructions for them. As expected, almost none read the more detailed information about the exhibit. Furthermore, the amount of enjoyment that visitors seemed to derive from playing with the exhibits was related to two factors: whether or not they read the instructions, and whether or not they worked with a partner. The most important contribution to the literature about science discovery rooms is that a majority of visitors did not simply manipulate the equipment randomly. Their actions at the exhibits showed that they understood the instructions; and their expressions showed that they were interested in what they discovered. An article on this aspect has also been published in the journal *Science Education*.

These qualities seem to make tabletop exhibits ideal for classroom learning stations. Ten of the most popular Wizard's Lab exhibits were selected to become a GEMS guide. These ten exhibits, along with the cartoon instructions, were among those included in the research study. As in the discovery room, we expect students will interact in teams of two or three to read the cartoon instructions and perform experiments on their own, which will lead to an understanding of various concepts in mechanics, electricity, and light. The potential for learning is even greater with a teacher who *will* read the more detailed information about the concepts, and who can lead a discussion with the whole class about what

they learned from each exhibit. We also developed a *Shapes, Loops, and Images* exhibit guide, with tabletop exhibits on shapes, reflections, and topology.

Building on the success of the *Wizard's Lab* and *Shapes, Loops, and Images* guides, successful teacher experience with learning stations in the classroom, and several of the most successful LHS school outreach programs, we developed other learning station GEMS guides, which are classroom-based, called "festivals." These include *Bubble Festival, Mystery Festival* and *Build It! Festival.* While the individual activities in all of these programs were not part of the *Wizard's Lab* study, they have undergone intense scrutiny and classroom testing by hundreds of teachers and the GEMS staff, and have been modified to enhance both educational effectiveness and presentation. The classroom learning station approach, because it allows students to proceed at their own pace, and make their own discoveries, can be a particularly effective way to present activity-based science and mathematics.

Conclusions

We examined three different kinds of research studies. The first was a pre- and post-test that showed the activities in the GEMS guide *Experimenting with Model Rockets* significantly improve students concepts of a controlled experiment, as well as their abilities to design, conduct, and critique the experiments of others. The second was an analysis of students' common misconceptions about astronomy. The results of that study formed the basis of the activities in the *Earth, Moon, and Stars* unit, which are designed to change those misconceptions by engaging students in observations of the sky, and to consider how alternative models can best explain their observations. The third study was a systematic observation of families in a science discovery room, which showed that children not only enjoy these activities, but also manipulate the materials correctly, indicating that they understand the concepts. Both interaction with others and cartoon-style directions turned out to be important factors in the success of learning stations.

While these various studies do not prove GEMS guides are more educationally effective than textbooks or other science programs, they are, we believe, compelling evidence that GEMS activities do what teachers strongly affirm they do— teach fundamental science concepts and skills, while providing students with stimulating and memorable experiences in science and math.

But please, let's **not** stop now! In our view, one of the most effective and relevant kinds of research is conducted by teachers to determine how effective the units are in improving their own students' understanding, abilities, and attitudes towards science and math. Suggestions for how to do this are given in many of the GEMS guides. The new GEMS assessment handbook, *Insights and Outcomes,* provides teachers with additional techniques for assessing their students' understandings and skills for all of the GEMS units. If you've developed your own methods for assessing student understanding, please let us know!

References

C. Sneider and S. Pulos. "Children's Cosmographies: Understanding the Earth's Shape and Gravity. "Science *Education* 67 (2) (1983): 205-221.

M. Erätuuli and C. Sneider. "The Experiences of Visitors in a Physics Discovery Room." *Science Education* 784 (4) (1990): 481-493.

C. Sneider, K. Kurlich, S. Pulos, A. Friedman. "Learning to Control Variables with Model Rockets: A Neo-Piagetian Study of Learning in Field Settings." *Science Education* 68 (4) (1984): 463-484.

1001 Ideas

to Promote
Activity-Based Science

*These ideas came from teacher/educator participants in
Great Explorations in Math & Science (GEMS) leadership workshops
held throughout the United States under a grant from the
National Science Foundation over a three-year period.*

*Many people contributed their time and expertise to the compilation of
these ideas, especially GEMS Center Coordinator Carolyn Willard,
GEMS Workshop Coordinator Laura Tucker, GEMS Principal Editor
Lincoln Bergman, GEMS Curriculum Specialist Cary Sneider,
GEMS Director Jacqueline Barber, and former
GEMS Administrative Coordinator Cynthia Ashley.*

Introducing 1001 Ideas

At every GEMS Leadership Workshop, we ask participants to discuss their ideas about what can be done to promote activity-based science and mathematics—not only GEMS—but **all** approaches that actively involve students in their learning. We recorded the ideas discussed during each workshop and present many of those ideas here. Please let us know if you find any of these ideas useful in your own educational efforts, or if you can suggest ways to expand on them.

We are all aware of the tremendous need for improved science and mathematics education nationwide. We know students learn best by doing, and that activity-based science and mathematics should be an integral part of any good curriculum. We have seen the enthusiasm and joy of learning that is generated by such an approach.

There are, of course, obstacles to presenting activity-based lessons. Sometimes we call them the NOT ENOUGHS—not enough funding, not enough preparation time, not enough space to store materials, not enough support from administrators and parents. What are some of the ways we can overcome these obstacles and make it possible for ALL students to enjoy and benefit from activity-based science and mathematics?—that is the question!

1001 Ideas range from quite easy and inexpensive ways to share GEMS and other activity-based curricula, to more elaborate, costly, and long-term efforts. They range from what we might dub "two-cent ideas," such as putting in your "two-cents" during conversations in the teacher's room or at the copy machine. A 20¢ idea might be calling a teacher-friend and sharing your enthusiasm for a favorite GEMS guide. For $2 you could buy two boxes of corn starch and make some "Oobleck," leaving it in the teacher's lounge with a sign asking: "what do you think this is?" For $20 you could buy some treats for a staff meeting and ask for 30 minutes to lead them in a hands-on activity. For $200, you might get substitutes for yourself and a colleague so you'd have time to set up a workshop for all fourth grade teachers in your district . . . and of course there's no limit to what you could come up with in the $2000 and more category! The important thing is that ALL these ideas, from 2 cents up, will help get more student hands on hands-on science and mathematics.

There is no best way of organizing ideas generated in over 100 brainstorming sessions in many states. However, any form of organization is useful in making sense of a wide range of data. Since GEMS users nationwide are organized into a network, we thought we would select a "network tree" as a way of organizing the ideas. At the center is the basic question: **What Can We Do to Promote Activity-Based Science and Mathematics?** The major branches of the network tree are the four main sections shown on the next page. The network is then expanded in outline form, with specific ideas listed, on the following pages.

While there is certainly plenty of overlap between these branches, and a fair amount of repetition, we felt it important to represent both the regional specificity and the richly diverse ways of expressing similar ideas, in the hope that a quite specific suggestion might help trigger novel ideas of your own, suited to your own unique situations. And there are some contradictory ideas.

This is a compendium of many viewpoints, and inclusion of an idea here does not necessarily imply its endorsement by the GEMS project, or ensure its feasibility. Lodged within are many pearls of wisdom gleaned from experience, helpful hints and brilliant "GEMS-like" flashes of insight.

We'd love to publish your comments and additions in a future issue of the *GEMS Network News,* and we also plan future revisions. Who knows—in time we may actually reach 1001 ideas—or even more!

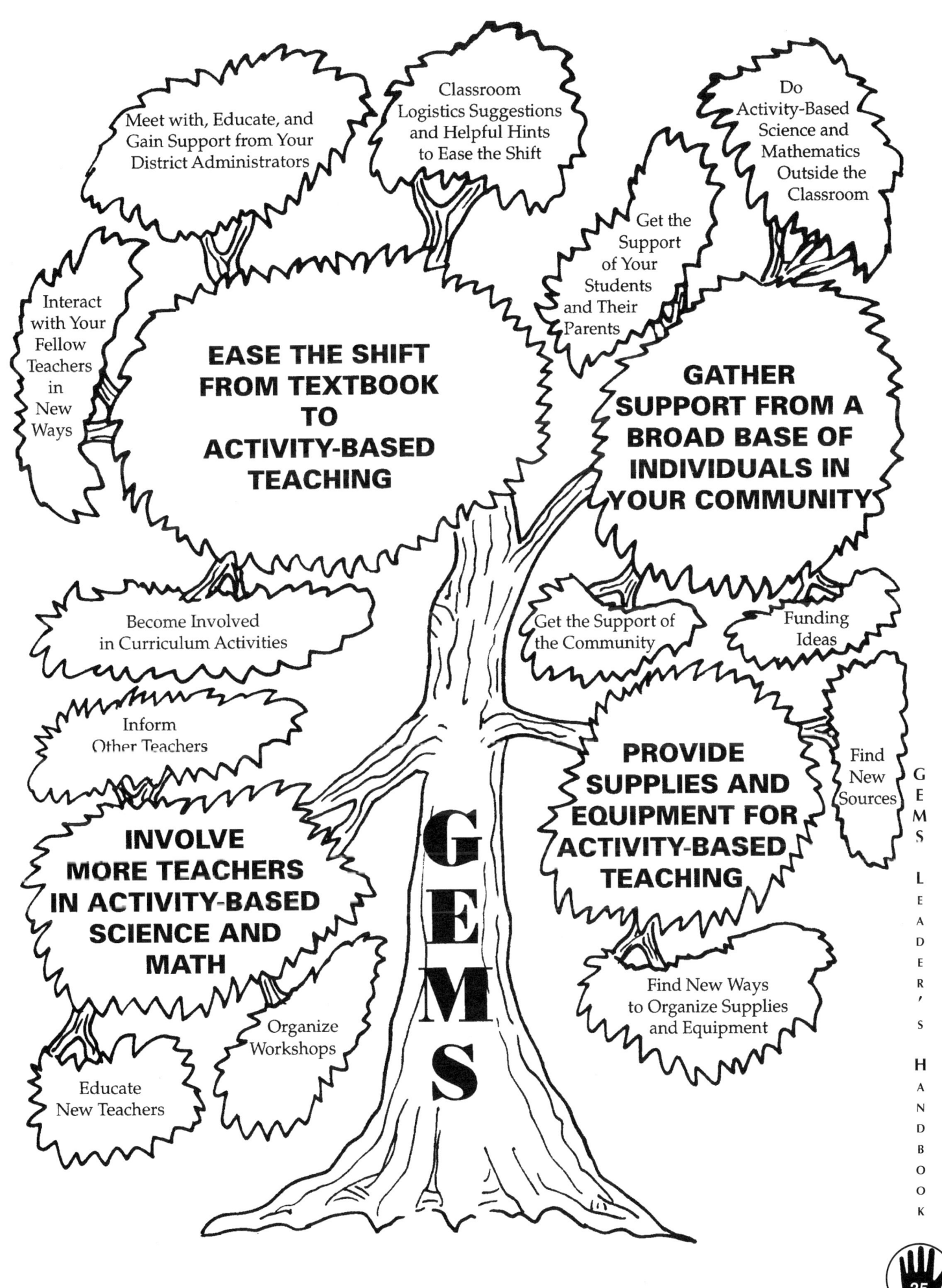

Involve More Teachers in Activity-Based Science and Mathematics

Inform Other Teachers

Getting other teachers excited about activity-based science is a good first step. Here are some suggestions on how to do that.

☞ Encourage teachers who are new to activity-based science and mathematics to begin with just one or two activities. Don't expect them to change their entire teaching style all at once.

☞ Share ideas at brown-bag lunches with science teachers in your school, or from neighboring schools.

☞ Organize a science/mathematics "swap meet," or "teachers' science fair," where teachers bring activities to share. Ideas can be demonstrated and written on paper, and/or computer disks.

☞ Hold an "invention convention" for teachers to share ideas for inexpensive science materials.

✎ Have your students write and publish articles about their science activities in the school newspaper or bulletin.

☞ Communicate with other teachers through electronic bulletin boards, especially those designed for science and mathematics educators, such as MIX.

✎ Write an article for a regional or state journal or newsletter about your experiences with GEMS, or workshops you have presented.

☞ Create GEMS posters, using work produced by your students, that can be put up in the teachers' rooms and at teachers' meetings.

☞ Communicate the advantages of activity-based science through any source possible, including: teacher supply stores, the Nature Company, bulletin boards, resource libraries, exhibit booths at county teacher meetings, sandwich boards, cablevision science programs, and skywriting!

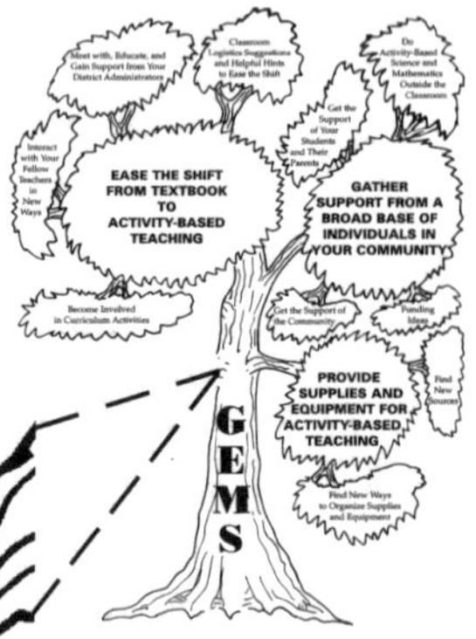

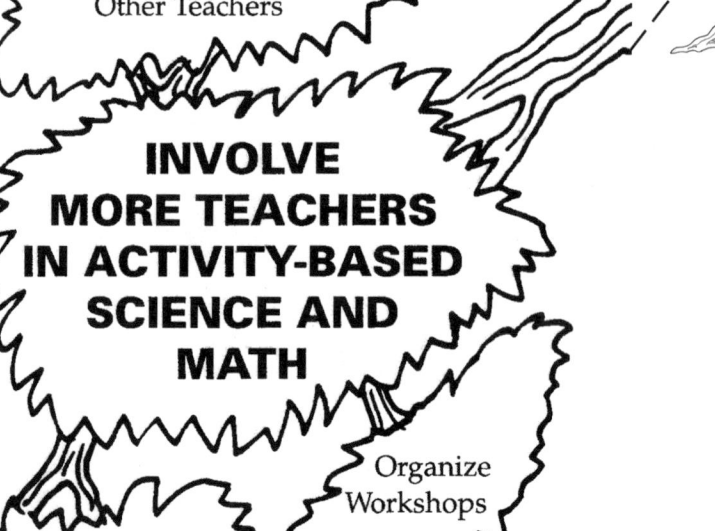

- Put up signs in your school about two weeks before conducting a science activity to generate interest. For example, "What Is Oobleck?" or "What is Bubble-ology?" The students' interest will generate teacher interest, and perhaps lead to some team teaching or at least sharing of ideas.

- Work to persuasively counter the often heard: "I am not a science person." (You don't have to be to teach a GEMS science or math unit!)

- Look for science connections to exciting programs already going on in your school. For example, the "Voyage of the Mimi" television series can be supplemented by GEMS activities from the guides *Mapping Animal Movements*, *Mapping Fish Habitats*, and *Liquid Explorations*.

- Explain to other teachers that emphasis on higher level thinking skills is consistent with oral language development, and with writing across the curriculum. Use Oobleck with teachers who say they are "not science people."

- One teacher co-authored an article in *Instructor* magazine on using literature connections to science and mathematics. Spread the word!

- Establish a teacher resource center at your local science center.

- Keep people informed through science association newsletters.

- Have once-a-month breakfasts with anyone interested in science for teachers to share ideas.

- Every Friday morning, have one faculty member share with others.

- Use GEMS video at district science curriculum meeting to inform others.

- Our school district newsletter has a hands-on science column.

- Run off a one-page idea for hands-on science on the copy machine—then leave some out with a sign: "Free: Take One!"

- Designate one person in the building to be the one who keeps track of workshops and outside resources, in addition to being expert on methods and materials—that person also becomes a communications expert.

- Designate *more than one* person to help be aware of workshops and opportunities.

- Make a time to share what you learned from an in-service with a friend.

- Share ideas at a grade level meeting (one successful activity or a favorite).

- Share your notes: rewrite them as you remember what you learned (your comments on likes, dislikes, etc., gives you a sense of "ownership").

- Share with curriculum specialists from the larger school system.

- To allay fears of staff members, invite teachers to view an activity. As you present it, they can see the mechanics and logistics.

- Find classrooms that have a one-way window viewer, so teachers can observe a lesson being done.

- Stress to District Supervisors within a state to carry the hands-on message to individual teachers.

- Set up a GEMS or other hands-on science/mathematics display at teacher's conventions.

- Go back to your schools and communicate. Put out your own newsletter. Hook people in and say "these are the people you can get in touch with."

☞ Key into blocks of content or themes teachers are already supposed to be presenting, reassuring them that they do not have to do more, but different.

☞ In Buffalo, we have a Teacher's Center. Contact your school district and see if they have something like that. We also have an excellent teacher's supply store where you can set up displays.

☞ Just as the "art consultant" comes, have a science consultant come and encourage the teachers.

☞ Get planning organized so the teacher can do it the night before, then save equipment/materials for the next year.

Tie in writing and reading for those teachers who don't like or have less experience in science.

☞ Make a videotape of a teacher presenting GEMS activities. Have a videotape library. Consider including videos and CD-ROMS that relate to the content of the guide, be it *River Cutters*, *Buzzing a Hive*, *Learning About Learning*, or *Moons of Jupiter*.

☞ Prepare handouts for sharing sessions in which each teacher shares one idea.

☞ See the evaluation section in the GEMS *Teacher's Handbook* and the section on correlation with state guidelines. They contain information that can be helpful when talking to other teachers.

☞ Get the word out through the publication "Superscience" published by Scholastic. There is an edition for primary and one for middle school.

☞ Share your successes with other teachers at a Share Fair. Get together—you'll have fun!

✎ Set up a newsletter or computer network between schools and classrooms. Promote what was successful.

☞ Science kits with videos that show exactly what to do, all materials that can stay in school or rotate through district.

☞ Have one lab teacher from each school come together with teachers from other schools to share ideas and materials.

☞ Teachers can team with another teacher.

✎ Chain letters to send people ideas about activities and workshops.

☞ Demonstrate how to teach a class with a teacher's students. Follow up by asking "When will you be doing a class next?" and offering to help or advise. It can help motivate a lot of people.

☞ Contact your science and mathematics methods teacher to let them know about GEMS.

✎ Submit articles to journals. If you have state teacher publications, get information out about GEMS.

☞ Take good advantage of informal teacher groupings: lunch groups, summer groups, etc.

☞ Resource teachers who go to other schools can spread the word.

☞ Develop a lead teacher to be in charge of GEMS dissemination in the district.

☞ Try just doing one activity. In my district we had one on electricity with batteries and bulbs and teachers just loved it! Once teachers see how much fun it is they become more open to hands-on activities.

- In the staff room have demonstrations and artifacts of GEMS activities; let people play with them.

- Model a GEMS activity for a teacher; try to get them to try it; give them support if they need you to come back. Until they take ownership for the kind of program that you are promoting, it won't happen. Give up some prep time; or get the principal to come in and cover for you.

- A couple of years ago, we had an Idea Swap—we picked one special thing we enjoyed doing as a lab or workshop, demonstrated it, and had a handout. I took home things that I continue to do. I was "psyched up" by what other people were doing. There were several teachers from all the junior high schools. First at school, then district, then regional.

- Publicity is important. Drop information on people's desks. Weekly meetings. Brown bag lunches to share activities. Resource centers.

- On a minimum day, have several teachers be preparing for a few different science lessons. Allow other teachers to cycle through, see what the activities involve and chat with them.

- Share GEMS guides. Give guides to teachers of other disciplines.

- Important for teachers learning about the hands-on approach to actually experience it, to get the excitement of hands-on learning and see you model how to present it to kids.

- Reassure teachers that it's okay to say "I've never done this before" with their kids.

- Put the results of projects in the school library.

- Distribute GEMS brochures and the teacher's handbook.

- Have the GEMS newsletter available in teacher's rooms, take photographs of students doing activities, give presentations or have a booth at county teacher conventions, present state-sponsored workshops from Department of Education.

- Encourage teachers within same school who use GEMS to make notes on what worked, their special management ideas, etc., and leave the notes in the back of an orientation manual for other teachers.

- In-service teachers will apply 15% of what they hear; but if someone comes into the classroom and models for them, they will utilize 85%.

- You must have hands-on learning for the teachers too—they will not read thick books either!

- Find a meeting time other than after-school with other teachers.

Teachers who are familiar with an activity can present something like *Oobleck* at a faculty meeting to get interdisciplinary ideas flowing.

- Let teachers **do** the activities and they'll see how non threatening and flexible GEMS activities are.

- In remote areas, use computers for communication.

- In a newsletter have a column for new ideas and for adaptations and offshoots from various GEMS activities.

☞ Show how GEMS and other activities can be directly related to state frameworks, thematic approaches, district guidelines, and more traditional curricula.
(Editor's note: Refer to the GEMS handbook, The Architecture of Reform, for ways to correlate GEMS to National Standards and other leading benchmarks and frameworks.)

☞ For teachers who are reluctant, explain that GEMS activities speak to:
1) critical thinking
2) changes (tangible to abstract)
3) cooperative learning
4) real-life applications
5) low cost
6) safety
7) all levels K–up
8) interdisciplinary
9) creativity

☞ Room can be crucial. Share with other teachers as needed to establish an arrangement that accommodates setup, team experimentation, class discussions. Enlist other teachers' help and offer the same to them.

☞ Hold a teacher appreciation day!

☞ Have GEMS loaner sets sent to show to the district. Send GEMS on approval and have the check torn up if materials are returned in good condition.
(Editor's Note: See page 78 for a form describing what the GEMS office can do for you.)

☞ GEMS activity guides make great holiday gifts. Handbooks too.

☞ Find out a particular teacher's interest and then suggest a science or math activity that connects to it.

☞ An enthusiastic teacher could take a small number of excited kids to share a great GEMS activity they did with kids in other classrooms.

☞ Tell others how and why a science workshop is worthwhile.

☞ Encourage fellow teachers to relax about presenting new things.

Teacher teams: help build kits together, think through lesson plans, get together after school.

☞ Have all-in-one meeting so teachers who teach the same grade level can see what others do, see what works, and get enthusiastic.

☞ Share hints for distribution of materials, such as sliding a paper plate under a piece of wax paper (for *Liquid Explorations*) or bringing around a bucket instead of carrying trays of water around the room, etc.

☞ Just **DO IT**!

✎ Write to the *GEMS Network News* with your ideas!!

Organize Workshops

The best way to introduce teachers to activity-based science and mathematics is through one or more workshops.

☞ Have teachers at your workshop actually **do** the activities, so they are excited and confident about how to do it.

☞ Emphasize simplicity of materials, low expense, ease of copying student sheets, and that previous science or math expertise is not essential to teach a good GEMS lesson.

☞ Plan a workshop for your fellow teachers during a regular after-school staff meeting, on a Saturday, or in the summer.

☞ Present a workshop for one hour before or after school. Ask your administrator to provide a stipend or "comp" time for teachers attending.

☞ Include a session on cooperative learning techniques as applied to science and mathematics.

☞ Work with administrators in your district to plan and present a workshop during a staff development day, or during summer orientation.

☞ Present a workshop at a teacher's conference in your local area, state, or region. Good conferences include state and national NSTA meetings, AAPT and ACS meetings, as well as state and national NEA meetings. Interdisciplinary uses of GEMS materials can be presented in workshops for teachers of English, Mathematics, Social Studies, Music and Art.

☞ Call a meeting of GEMS Associates or Leaders in your state to plan workshops together. *(There are GEMS Leaders and Associates in every state!)* Contact the GEMS National Office for more information on Associates near you.

☞ Contact your State Science or Mathematics Supervisor for advice on when and where you can present GEMS workshops.

☞ Contact the nearest science center to see if they will host a workshop. They may be able to help with space, supplies, equipment, and publicity for a workshop.

☞ When arranging a workshop, request that funds from the district science/mathematics budget purchase copies of GEMS guides for the teachers who attend. Thus, each teacher can receive a detailed description of the activity, materials and preparation, background, additional resources, and extension activities.

✍ Write a proposal to the National Science Foundation, or your State Department of Education, to conduct a Summer Institute for one or more weeks so teachers will have experience doing all of the GEMS activities at their grade level, and can share ideas about how these activities will help them meet their teaching objectives.

☞ Apply for Title II staff development funds to support workshop programs.

✍ Call or write to GEMS Headquarters at the Lawrence Hall of Science to borrow (or purchase) the GEMS videotape for use at your workshop. Duplicate these materials for future workshops if you wish. If borrowing, pay only for return postage.
(Editor's Note: See page 78 for a form describing what the GEMS office can do for you.)

☞ Conduct GEMS workshops at your school that will interest the English, Mathematics, Social Studies, and other teachers by emphasizing the extensions of activities to other subject areas. They can present GEMS activities in their classes, or present lessons that complement GEMS activities presented in science or mathematics classes.
(Editor's Note: Share a copy of the GEMS literature handbook, Once Upon A GEMS Guide: Connecting Young People's Literature to Great Explorations in Math and Science, *with English teachers.)*

Present one activity *fully* (with direct participant involvement) rather than *talking about* several activities. If your group of teachers learns only two or three good activities a year, after several years they will have a large repertoire of activities to present.

☞ Videotape your own students doing science/mathematics activities, and show portions of the video at a workshop, after the participants have done that activity themselves.

☞ Invite other teachers who are involved in activity-based science to share the work of planning and conducting a workshop. In general, just as with students and cooperative learning, working together helps things come out better. Constructively debrief after each workshop, so all presenters can improve their skills.

☞ Good organizational skills are important. Ask for help from colleagues who have done workshop organizing before (sometimes known as "Conference Junkies"). Professional workshop organizers can also be very helpful.

☞ Whenever possible, workshop instructors should be teachers since they have firsthand experience in presenting/managing science and mathematics activities in the classroom.

☞ Invite high school and middle school science and mathematics teachers to present workshops on activity-based teaching for elementary teachers. They can emphasize the vital role of elementary teachers in developing students' skills in observing, experimenting, and drawing conclusions. Perhaps they can allay some nervousness when elementary teachers become aware of what these upper level teachers are already doing.

☞ Invite retired teachers, who are experienced in hands-on methods, to model good activity-based teaching at workshops, or to help new teachers in their classrooms.

☞ Make contact with a college professor who can help provide college credit for teachers who attend in-service workshops.

☞ Allow time for teachers in a workshop to brainstorm extensions of activities. Thus, the activities form a springboard for discussion, so the teachers become more involved in using the activities to meet their own objectives.

☞ Give teachers who have had several workshops the opportunity to develop their own science and mathematics activities, so the activity-based approach becomes an integral aspect of their teaching style.

☞ Whenever possible, follow up on workshops by visiting school sites and helping teachers who want to present activity-based science.

☞ Identify teacher educators in your area who have not had an opportunity to learn about the GEMS program. Design a special workshop for them.

☞ Set up technical information centers, with city or other funds, to pay for 2,000 days of substitute service. Teachers come to three full-day workshops each; all fifth grade teachers one year, all fourth grade teachers the next, so eventually all grade levels get three full days of training. Give out GEMS guides **and** materials.

☞ Two-hour workshops for teacher assistants are very helpful.

Have everything at the workshop that the teacher needs to take to do the activity in the classroom the next day, that is, the teacher's guide and all materials. Requisitions take forever! The value of a workshop can be measured by whether or not it can be taken into the classroom the very next day.

☞ During in-service time have interdepartmental meetings, so science people in the building can share with each other.

☞ In California, we have a mentorship program. It's a great help to get teachers from your school to attend.

☞ Science Mentors can disseminate GEMS. There are two Science Mentors in our district. But, don't cut this short by calling it "science." It should include math, certainly! The Mentor Program includes teachers identified as exceptional, well-versed, and able to communicate skills to new teachers.

☞ Organize a small group of interested teachers; have someone in the district present hands-on activities to the interested group, so they can spread the word. The district initially only needs to pay for eight substitutes or so.

☞ For in-service teacher education, make sure districts "buy into it" by purchasing the GEMS guides, so when teachers leave the workshop, they have the materials to take to their schools.

☞ In New York, we have teacher centers run by and for teachers. To empower the teachers, have teachers teach each other.

☞ Offer GEMS workshops through a Special Education Training Resource Center. GEMS could be used for special education, which is too often left out in the cold.

☞ Some community colleges may not be official teacher training institutions, but you can still arrange to present classes there, for non-credit continuing education.

☞ Sometimes science activity books have wonderful ideas, but they still tend to sit on the shelf. Workshops are the key. Most things I go back and actually do in class are the things we did in workshops.

☞ Eisenhower Higher Education funds controlled by State agencies are available for college level courses/workshops.

☞ Often independent (private) school teachers don't hear about workshops such as GEMS. I see that as a gap. We still all teach kids and want to get kids excited about science and math. If any of you know of anyone who teaches at a private school, please share with them. We do get left out a lot of the time.

☞ Make inexpensive kits for teachers to take back from a workshop. Call it a "make and take" workshop. Buy materials in quantity. As they do an activity, they shove their materials into their bags and take them home.

☞ Ask for support from administrators (and custodians!); ask for in-service workshops with later follow-up sessions to support and encourage teachers after they try the activities.

☞ Have an all-day workshop for a particular grade level, with substitutes brought in.

☞ In doing teacher workshops, I find that if you can give out materials, even simple and inexpensive ones, teachers are more apt to use the activities.

☞ Once you get an idea, have an informal workshop and share it with your colleagues!

☞ Make sure your in-service is fun.

☞ Get involved in new hands-on science activities, like BSCS. Get into an institute/workshop that offers a stipend.

☞ Plan and present a **series** of workshops—tie them together around a particular theme or approach.

☞ Feature GEMS at staff development day. Use staff meetings for in-service education. Put "administrivia" into a bulletin and use meeting time better.

☞ Conduct staff development in neighboring school districts.

☞ Coordinate with local and regional science teaching organizations.

☞ Countywide training—all meet at the science center.

☞ Team teachers together so they can support each other— peer teachers who are especially good at different units.

☞ Salary points for workshops should be available for teachers to go to next salary step.

☞ In Pittsburgh, we have Summer Science Academy where teachers come to see how hands-on activities work with 15 people— before you try it with 30 kids.

☞ Attend or present workshops at NASDA-sponsored events, NSTA state meetings, state education association conventions, local education meetings.

☞ Establish a college credit course/workshop for teachers, examining/critiquing several science/math programs, for example, GEMS, Family Math, NSRC, AIMS, etc.

☞ Utilize and reach teachers on sabbatical.

☞ Provide workshops for home school people.

☞ Share ideas and activities at regional museum-related conferences.

☞ Hold a teacher camp-in.

☞ Have a preschool teacher in-service workshop.
(Editor's Note: Several GEMS guides are excellent for preschoolers, such as Ladybugs and Tree Homes from the PEACHES series, and more are on the way.)

☞ Present after-school courses for teachers. If we have the money we pay a training rate for participants and hire the instructors. We offer courses of two hours per week for ten weeks. We also have people going to workshops in schools for released half-days, other times lunch hours are added to extend prep periods.

☞ Saturday Science program. Teachers from all over the city are invited to attend hands-on workshops and pick up materials. We have teachers, instructors, and even commercial groups doing workshops. We reach a large group of teachers in the city.

☞ The Science Council of New York has a conference, about 500–600 teachers. If we had GEMS materials we could present GEMS there.

☞ Drive-in conference on Saturday morning: Teacher brings someone from school who does not do discovery activities. Non-inquiry teacher will go home a little more confident and convinced.

☞ At workshops, tell people about many curricula: FOSS, Project Wild, etc.

☞ Professional development committees, open to K–12 teachers: could be used for an in-service workshop.

☞ Mini-workshops, parent involvement, invite teachers, have kids do roving demonstrations.

☞ Use *Crime Lab Chemistry* to introduce "science as mystery" at a workshop.

☞ Two weeks in-service in the summer—week 1: workshops for teachers; week 2: teach to kids.

☞ Distribute GEMS brochures at your workshops. "Here is the best bargain in the world."

☞ Our school has a grant through the state college system to take teachers from the math department for one full day four times a year. This year, it was done for half the department at a time. If I can bring some of these GEMS materials to the person who is running these workshops, that will be very helpful.

☞ Some districts provide in-services to teachers then give them materials already in a box. Teachers return box and the district replenishes it.

☞ Present GEMS workshops for teachers of gifted and talented kids.

☞ Give Advanced Academic Credit (AAT) workshops (teacher credits for merit pay).

☞ Arrange for student teachers to take over classes so regular teachers can attend hands-on science workshops.

☞ Develop a training program at a local elementary school to provide teachers with more experience in hands-on presentation. Expand to include additional schools.

☞ Have teachers bring last week's or last year's lesson plans to a workshop, and see how they might have done it differently with GEMS techniques.

✍ Write to the *GEMS Network News* with your ideas!!

Educate New Teachers

Preservice education has the advantage of developing new habits in teachers who are just starting out.

☞ Contact your local college or graduate school of education. Offer to present workshops to pre-college teachers in activity-based science, including GEMS and other effective and tested programs.

✍ Write proposals to develop new activity-based science and mathematics methods courses at colleges.

Develop ways to ensure that direct experience in hands-on science and math becomes a consistent, key, and required part of student teacher training and education department course offerings.

☞ Introduce college students to activity-based mathematics and science by doing an involving activity. Have them do one of the "going furthers," or research some of the references and resources included in GEMS guides. Show the changes in educational theory and approach that have led to the present.

☞ Send out GEMS brochures and/or GEMS guides to college education professors, especially those who teach methods classes.

☞ Identify and select master teachers who *do* activity-based science to help train new teachers.

☞ Be certain that new teachers have opportunities to **present** activities (not simply observe them) so they will gain confidence and enthusiasm.

☞ Train preservice teachers in hands-on math and science activities, so they can model presentations for teachers who did not get that training and currently teach science from a textbook or not at all.

☞ Organize an internship program that emphasizes hands-on activities.

☞ Organize a small in-service for new teachers, to acquaint them with hands-on activity-based science and mathematics.

☞ Spend lots of time doing activities in preservice classes, so more hands-on, rather than lecturing, is modeled and learned. Research shows that we tend to teach in the way we were taught.

☞ Videotape students doing experiments—send to college education students.

✍ Write to the *GEMS Network News* with your ideas!!

Provide Supplies and Equipment for Activity-Based Teaching

Find New Sources of Supplies and Equipment

✍ Write letters to parents, asking them to save various items such as baby food jars, milk cartons, etc. This can be done during the school year as equipment is needed, or with one letter at the beginning of the year, listing a wide range of materials that you will need. Set up collection boxes in the room to serve as visual reminders for parents and kids. *(Editor's Note: A number of GEMS guides include sample letters to parents requesting donations of materials for that unit.)*

☞ Contact local businesses to contribute supplies and equipment to your classroom, or to the district science resource center. Give them credit in the local newspaper, so other businesses will donate as well.

☞ Have a local company "adopt a school." They can provide funds, supplies and equipment, volunteers to prepare materials and assist in the classroom, and possibly experts on various subjects to address your students.

☞ Ask for business/corporate contributions of funds to purchase specialized science and mathematics supplies and equipment.

☞ Check with your local college mathematics or science professors to see if they can loan equipment or give you surplus materials.

☞ See if your state has a surplus supplies warehouse, for use by state agencies and schools.

☞ Ask a science center or museum if they can provide loaner kits. Offer assistance in writing proposals so that science centers can get funds to provide the kits free of charge to local schools.

☞ Arrange for purchases to be done through charge accounts at local stores, such as hardware stores, grocery stores, etc.

☞ Use community resources such as agricultural assistance labs, soil testing agencies, weather stations, etc. When possible, invite people into the classroom to discuss their expertise and the ways their careers involve math and science.

☞ Use software related to GEMS activities. For example, a simulation of a titration in chemistry would go nicely with *Vitamin C Testing*. A simulated trip to Mars could be used in conjunction with *Oobleck: What Do Scientists Do?*

☞ Take advantage of public domain software that you can receive from electronic bulletin boards.

☞ Plan a mini-field trip around the school yard, using materials that are right there.

☞ Go through all the cabinets to find things people aren't using and put them in a central place so people can know they're there.

☞ Share the task of gathering materials with other teachers. Pass the materials around to each other.

☞ At my school we have lots of scientific equipment. We provide a list of what we have to other teachers at other schools for loaning. When a teacher come to borrow something, a word of advice can be shared too.

☞ Have parents be resource people both to help teach and provide materials.

☞ In one school teachers use Pepsi bottles to make thermometers, and then send pictures of it to Pepsi.

☞ Let parents buy and put together the kits. Principals could send out purchase orders to the places where the items can be purchased.

☞ Have students go door-to-door to collect materials; such as two-liter bottles. Even people who do not have children might be interested, so the whole community could contribute. This would also be valuable for community folks to find out what is going on in the schools.

☞ Some science supply companies produce videos, showing you how to get everything together—these are much better than reading it alone. They show the set up of the trays, equipment, etc.

☞ For long-term buying: get parent volunteer to run through lists, see what materials are, and organize buying trips.

☞ Some groups have pre-vocational workshops and can make things, for example, Wizard's Lab exhibits. Maybe a high school shop class could help out.

☞ Instead of buying textbooks for all students in the school, use the funds saved to buy more science equipment.

☞ Collect a lab fee from the kids each week (10 cents) to buy the cinnamon, bananas, other materials, etc.

✌ Have a display of intriguing materials, with a sign saying, "Ask me!"

☞ Have a central location for science supplies, with a person in charge, to be sure that the equipment is all there.

- More make-it-and-take-it workshops!

- Feature a list of needed materials in the school newspaper.

- Get school district administrators to build a special fund into the budget for perishable items that cannot be stored in the science closet all the time.

- Use simple materials, as few as possible—this makes it easier for the teacher.

- Backs of magazines sometimes offer stuff for free.

- Kids can contribute some of the supplies too.

- Go to a big supermarket and set up a booth with hands-on activities, showing what neat things you do in your science program. Feature activities that use grocery supplies (dishwashing liquid, Kosher salt, starch, baby oil, etc.). Ask people if they might donate one of these items on their way out.

- Science mother/father helpers are parents who go out and collect the materials and put them in one spot. Eventually they help to organize the materials.

- All teachers get together and have a science shop day to prepare materials.

- "Bottle Biology." There are hundreds of activities you can do with 2-liter bottles. For more information on these great activities, call (608) 263-5645 or write:
    Fast Plants/Bottle Biology
    University of Wisconsin
    Department of Plant Pathology
    1630 Linden Drive
    Madison, WI 53706

- One elementary teacher had her students collect 1,000,000 pop tops. They took them to a recycling center and donated money to purchase science equipment.

- Get a cart to move materials.

- Use cardboard soda pop boxes as distribution trays.

- Many supplies can be recycled materials.

- Explain to parents that their kids' experiences will be much fuller if they give donations, either money or equipment. Just asking for donations is usually successful.

- Do presentations at the PTA for parents to be aware of the need for materials.

Have a "Science Shower" like a wedding shower, but for science!

- Develop a relationship with a butcher—get free Styrofoam trays, liver containers, etc. Sometimes just mentioning that you're a teacher is enough.

- Plan to concentrate teaching in a time period that allows all materials to be distributed and used to complete the activity, rather than having to stop in the middle, reorganize and redistribute materials the next day, etc.

- Do buying in bulk, from catalogs, large discount outlets, etc.

- Check to see if the school district warehouse has supplies.

Get free stuff from grocery stores, lumber stores, sewing stores, recyclers. Optometrists have small glass bottles with plastic lids (contact lenses). Florists donate old flowers free.

- Have a bake sale.

☞ Announce or post a "Materials Wish List" at Back to School night.

☞ Locate old, discarded science kits to recycle materials. Go to your Instructional Materials Center and find kits purchased for other programs. Often they are not even opened. For example, I found a "Concepts in Science" kit from the 1950s and found lots of ways to use those materials.

☞ I offer extra credit to my students if they bring in old tools, slides, etc.

☞ Get balance scales from police department (confiscated from drug busts).

☞ Get medicine droppers and small plastic cough medicine cups from your druggist.

☞ Supply list for annual budget should include science supplies.

Have a potluck science party. Use large boxes, one for each teacher. Post a list of materials for a specific activity and have people bring things for it. At the party, you could "brainstorm" a list of places to get things—parents who are nurses may have basins or tongue depressors, and so on.

☞ Have a wish list on your board. Even lasers or TVs will sometimes appear!

☞ Have a "Treasure Hunt" theme at the beginning of the year with a list of needed materials.

☞ Hold a science fair. Then, after involving parents, hold a fund-raiser for the science lab.

✍ Apply for grants for supplies from, for example, NSTA, License Plate Grant (California), local corporate/business assistance.

✍ Write to the *GEMS Network News* with your ideas!!

Find New Ways to Organize Supplies and Equipment

☞ Share the work of developing kits which then can circulate to other classes or other schools.

☞ Organize purchases into a large "buying trip." Use parent volunteers to help you shop.

☞ Create a "Science Resource Center" at your school or school district, where science supplies and equipment can be stored. Involve a teacher or parent volunteer to maintain the center, who will check and replenish kits, repair equipment, maintain teacher sign-up lists, and transport kits to classrooms where and when they are needed.

☞ Districts could have a centralized kit system. Teachers request kits, pick them up and return for restocking.

☞ Set up a resource closet. This might have a shelf of "fasteners," containers, tools—general supplies that all teachers can use. Ask all at school to help stock the closet. Sometimes you just need one dumb little thing—you forgot your potato peeler at home.

☞ Maintain a resource file on science activity guides and kits in your school building. File according to recommended grade levels, topic and/or theme.

☞ Store equipment for each unit in a "banker's box," labeled, with a lid and a list of all materials in it, and additional consumable materials that must be purchased for each lesson. Put the relevant GEMS guide inside the box.

- ☞ Use large plastic tubs to store lots of materials. Tubs with covers can be stacked, or slide them onto shelves in a storage closet or along the wall.

- ☞ Shoe boxes, baskets, and ziplock plastic bags are good ways of organizing smaller materials, or making kits for small groups of students.

- ☞ Plan a volunteer parent's work day, so kits can be prepared for several science units in advance.

- ☞ Maintain a library of videotapes showing teachers at your school doing different GEMS activities, for use by new teachers in training, to give them a sense of classroom dynamics and management.

- ☞ Create science exhibits for students to play with at recess and lunchtime, using ideas from the GEMS exhibit guides, *Shapes, Loops, and Images* and *The Wizard's Lab*, and from learning station "festival" guides, such as *Bubble Festival, Mystery Festival,* and *Build It! Festival*.

- ☞ Get help from high school shop teachers to produce science exhibits and other science materials.

- ☞ Once all materials are purchased, provide release-time to set up kits for the units.

- ☞ To avoid losing the activity directions, put the guide in the box of materials or tape directions to the box, with a source to buy replacement materials. You need a master copy, too.

- ☞ Have your school district hire someone to help teachers organize materials, or use community volunteers.

- ☞ Have different teachers in the same grade level share equipment.

- ☞ Assemble kits by units that are taught in the school system.

- ☞ Use parent volunteers as helpers, helping kids get materials on trays.

- ☞ Have more teacher-made science kits with the data sheets duplicated, etc. If other teachers saw us pulling the kits from the storage room, and found out the materials were already together, they'd be more willing to try.

- ☞ Set up a resource room with useful junk: coke bottles, baby food jars, etc.

- ☞ Provide science kits: ziplock bags with what each student needs so it will be there at their fingertips.

- ☞ Things to make it easier for teachers—prepackaged kits. Hard stuff to find should be in a kit. Organize and label so teachers know what they're teaching.

- ☞ Calibrate your own measuring devices, so you can use ordinary containers rather than more expensive graduated cylinders.

- ☞ Have central checkout points in the district to check out equipment that is too expensive to have at each school.

- ☞ Make a designated, accessible resource room where science supplies can be kept, with a sign-out list, organized boxes, etc.

- ☞ Ask the children to help you organize your materials. The kids are often very anxious to help you, and if you have the patience, it is great!

- ☞ Use tubs of materials for team teaching: one teacher sets up one unit, another teacher another—teachers become specialists in certain units.

☞ In each grade level, we have one person in charge of science, including having supplies ordered, put into box, with copy of the experiment and make sure it gets around to all other teachers in that grade.

☞ Have some "at-home kits" in the library for student checkout.

☞ In a self-contained classroom, you often do not have a place to put things; build a science cart, so that everything is there. Let other teachers borrow it. Get a carpenter to donate time, have a store or parent donate a couple of pieces of plywood, etc.

☞ Take turns setting up materials for an experiment. Biggest hassle is the set up. Sometimes you don't have time to do that. So, take turns and let other people use the setup the next day or next week. Let those materials travel all over the building.

☞ Each district should have a supply of bulk materials and equipment to check out. Hold an open-house for teachers to go through the materials and see what's there.

☞ If building a new school be sure you have a **storeroom**.

☞ Simplify the number of items you have to collect.

☞ Senior citizens could help with equipment and experiments.

☞ Putting a number on each piece of equipment indicates ownership, and helps in getting it back.

☞ Baskets, shoe boxes, trays, and ziplock bags are useful to help get organized before doing a unit. Each child can then get one bag or box of materials for their table.

☞ Use plastic trash bag aprons to protect furniture and kids.

☞ Students can be "lab technicians" to help teachers pick up supplies, label cups, and do other things that would otherwise stop teachers from doing experiments.

☞ Parents can do assembly of stuff. A parent has been doing that for my class, and she's become an advocate for science as well. She can also be loaned to another classroom, since she now has experience in putting science kits together.

☞ Early retirement people could organize donations of materials.

☞ Laminate activity cards, signs for learning stations, etc.

☞ The PTA could put together kits in grade-level boxes, correlated to the State Science Framework.

Write to the *GEMS Network News* with your ideas!!

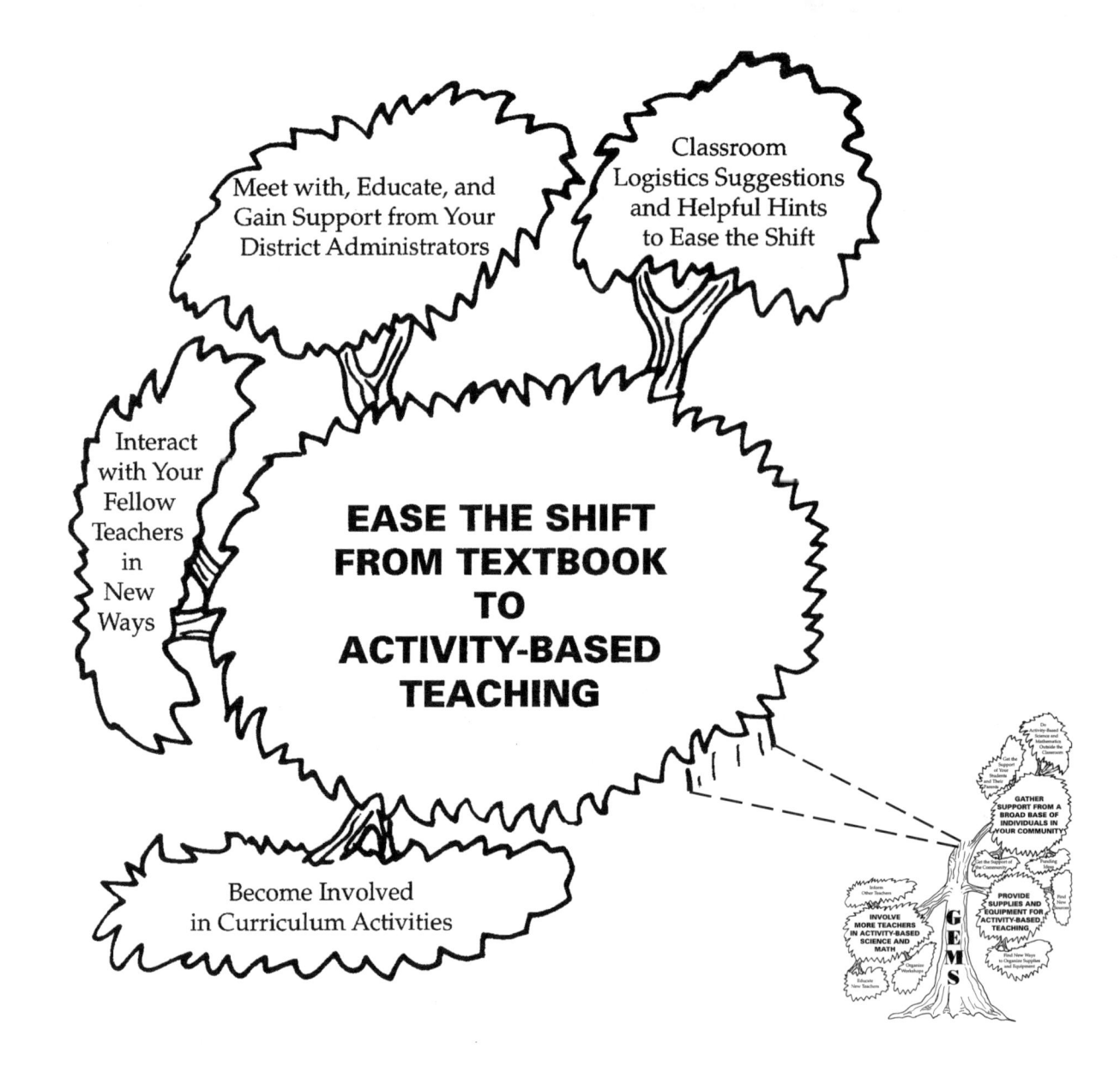

Ease the Shift from Textbook to Activity-Based Teaching

Interact with Your Colleagues in New Ways

☞ Team teach with other science teachers by each presenting your favorite activities to each other's classes, and by helping each other during class activities where the "mess quotient" is high.

☞ Create a teaching team involving both mathematics and science teachers, so that you can teach mathematics skills through relevant science problems.

☞ Adopt an interdisciplinary approach. Select a broad topic for the week for your school or grade level, such as "Bubble Week." Have teachers in all classes present lessons relating to that topic.

☞ Create science teaching teams involving English teachers, bilingual teachers, Social Studies, Art, and Music teachers. Emphasize the interdisciplinary nature of science by inventing lessons that accomplish objectives across the curriculum.

☞ Focus activities on a "Scientist of the Week," including lessons about the time period when he or she lived, the person's location, their work, and its consequences. Don't forget women and minority scientists, and the international nature of scientific work.

☞ Use GEMS activities for Special Education students, **since they can all have success.**

☞ Adapt materials so they are easy for young children, such as making extra large finger-prints, or pre-labeling containers.

☞ Extend activities, so they are challenging for gifted and talented students and high school students.

☞ Use GEMS activities with high-risk students, to help keep them interested in school.

☞ Incorporate *Crime Lab Chemistry*, *Finger-printing*, and *Mystery Festival* with units on crime prevention, and teaching about careers in law enforcement.

☞ Use GEMS activities, such as *Vitamin C Testing*, in units on nutrition, and/or consumer science.

☞ Work with other teachers at your school to organize a science fair. Use GEMS activities such as *Paper Towel Testing* as examples of good science fair projects, to get the students started on their own projects.

☞ During a science fair, have tables with activities from *Bubble-ology*, *Crime Lab Chemistry*, and *Oobleck* set up, so that students and their parents can **do** science investigations.

☞ Hold a "Science Circus" with activities such as *Animals in Action*, and *The Magic of Electricity*.

☞ Hold a "Science Awareness Day" with displays and speakers on science careers and lessons on the role of science in everyday life. Have students do activities from *Vitamin C Testing* or *Paper Towel Testing*, which relate to both careers and daily living.

☞ Allow for "Electives," when students may choose their classes for one or more weeks. Provide fun science and mathematics topics for them to choose from, such as "Animal Investigations," or "Science In the Crime Lab."

☞ Have classes or schools compete in science contests, such as designing the most original shuttlecraft for navigating across an ocean of "Oobleck."

☞ Hold a "Science Olympiad," where students meet challenges, such as layering liquids (from the GEMS guide *Discovering Density*) in a short time period.

☞ If your school has self-contained classes, and other teachers will not do activity-based science, consider becoming a "traveling science teacher" and present science to all of the students in your school.

Enrich your science and mathematics classes by presenting poetry and art related to the topics you are teaching.

☞ Trade classes so each teacher can teach what he or she does best. That way students receive activity-based science and mathematics from teachers who enjoy teaching that way.

If your school has many bilingual students, ask bilingual teachers to assist you in leading science discussions in other languages, so all students can participate. Ask students to translate for other students.

☞ Since science requires supplies and equipment, sinks and tables, try to get administrative support for a special science classroom at your school which will be visited by other classes.

☞ Use the school cafeteria to teach science, since there is water available and tables for conducting experiments.

☞ Arrange for science teachers to substitute extra prep periods for lunch duty, since some activity-based science requires a lot of preparation.

☞ Have older students present activities to younger students in small groups.

☞ Cooperate with schools across the country to compare fingerprints or paper towel testing results. Use the mail or computer bulletin boards for this.

☞ Train high school students in GEMS activities. Have them present lessons in middle and elementary schools.

☞ Some school districts have closed-circuit television or satellite transmission. Broadcast the GEMS Assembly Presenters' Guides, such as *Solids, Liquids, and Gases*, or *Magic of Electricity*.

✎ Our district has a newsletter with our instructional objectives for each grade level: reading, math, science, etc., sent to the schools every six weeks. Feature GEMS guides as they relate.

☞ As an administrator, I know that if one or two teachers start an activity that gets the kids interested, other teachers start asking about it.

☞ Be creative with the space you have—cooperate with other rooms, such as art (with sinks) so when it's not used for art it can be used as a science room. Shop and home economics rooms work well too.

☞ Set up an activity in one classroom, then have more than one class do the activity there by trading rooms. This saves multiple effort for setup and cleanup.

☞ Exchange with another teacher—she takes your kids for music, you take hers for science.

☞ Get librarian, Physical Education, and music teachers involved in GEMS activities. (Bee dances in *Buzzing a Hive*, short dramas in many GEMS guides, literature connections, etc.)

Incorporate lessons on other cultures, such as the "Mythological Models of the World" activity in the GEMS guide, *Earth, Moon, and Stars*. or the activities in *Investigating Artifacts*.

☞ One science teacher started a science club for 4th–5th graders. She calls the club "The Detectives." They spent an entire semester on GEMS Crime Lab and Fingerprinting activities, plus follow-ups, and next semester will be on bubbles.

☞ With teachers working in teams, it's more difficult for those who avoid science to hide. Stay together and science ends up being fun.

☞ Science specialists are helpful. Management of materials is very difficult for the self-contained teacher.

- Put all different activities on computer disks, easy to store. CD ROM? Call up all activities that will fit your concepts or processes. Bring your own disk to swap shop, plus blank disks to copy other people's programs. It takes a long time to learn enough activities, since they are not in textbooks.

- Share with special education teachers within the building.

- Teachers with talent in second languages should do some reporting in the other language. This would be a nice addition to a multicultural group. One of our schools has 96 different languages represented in the student body!

- Using a computer to communicate with other schools and communicate about science and math. Scientific convention in Oobleck can be done with other schools, and even other districts.

- Share with students in other countries. A school in California is in contact with a school in Russia via the TERC Kid's Net.

- Have a short after-school workshop demonstrating some activities with students while other teachers watch.

- "Divvy" up the science book or curriculum so each teacher is responsible for a different box of materials and lesson plans.

- Colleagues team-plan, share ideas; for example, two teachers, one does math/science the other language/social studies. Teachers plan their subjects for a week, then share.

- Have math-science team meetings at middle school to coordinate how to use and combine math and science teaching opportunities in GEMS activities.

- Help teachers see the "buried" math and language arts in science.

- It's much more efficient to set up, for example, "Liquid Explorations" for more than one class and have students rotate. This helps with set up and clean up efficiency. If a teacher is comfortable with a particular unit; other teachers on the same grade level would know it is his specialty and he can help with pitfalls. Next door, another unit is available with its expert, etc. That way each person does not have overwhelming responsibility.

- Maybe take measurement responsibility out of math and give it to science teacher or share with other areas of the curriculum.

- One day a month have a roving substitute so you can help present/peer teach activities.

- Coach teachers in how to efficiently team teach. Teachers try and fail and therefore don't do it anymore. Teaching to their strengths really helps teams succeed.

Have English classes write the scenarios for *Crime Lab Chemistry*.

- Share teach Oobleck: Let one teacher do the lab part, and another can do the convention part so they're working with their strengths.

- Small districts can pool money and coordinate as multiple districts. They can have cluster meetings, so representatives from each district can go.

- Take materials out of the classroom and do activities so they become visible; or install a glass wall in your classroom so other teachers and students can see what you're doing. "They're having more fun than we are!"

☞ Build a synergistic, very creative team approach. For example, two teachers take the entire group for a water and air unit, culminating with a water and air magic show. Another team would prepare a unit for the whole school for the next week, like measuring everyone in the school and making graphs. That is a really different approach to team teaching.

✍ Write to the *GEMS Network News* with your ideas!!

Become involved in curriculum committees

☞ Meet with other science and mathematics teachers in your school to review the state and local guidelines for teaching science and mathematics.

☞ Create a "map" showing how the science and mathematics activities address the goals and objectives or essential elements described in state and local guidelines.

☞ Work with other teachers in your school to plan topics and activities for every grade, so students will not repeat activities and concepts and will build their knowledge from year to year.

☞ Identify GEMS units with an emphasis on mathematics, and inform your district's mathematics curriculum committee. Do the same with units that relate to English, Social Studies, or Art.

☞ When adopting textbooks, consider programs such as GEMS instead of standard textbook programs.

☞ Ask the curriculum coordinator in your area to integrate GEMS activities with existing textbooks.

Use the information on the first page of each GEMS teacher's guide to relate the concepts, skills, and themes taught by that unit to the objectives of state and local guidelines, or to the scope and sequence of a particular textbook series. (*Editor's Note: The GEMS* Teacher's Handbook *includes a chart showing skills, concepts, and themes for all the GEMS guides.*)

☞ Bring information and/or do presentations at the math and science curriculum committee.

☞ At each school have grade level meetings for teachers to correlate and plan activities.

☞ Work through an elementary science curriculum committee.

☞ Before we have activity-based science, we've got to have time for science, period. We proposed a District Management system—a calendar of topics for testing, with student profile sheets to monitor each child. This helped ensure that teachers taught science and on a frequent enough basis. We had 96% completion of all topics.

☞ Correlate GEMS activities to existing state and local curriculum guides.

☞ Develop units of study, incorporating science into other curricula.

☞ For GEMS units, I've marked the grade level and the essential element of the activity that satisfies requirements of the state of Texas. This will help teachers correlate this with what they are required to teach.

☞ Hold a symposium for parents, and for those who have handed down a curriculum—they can change their minds. At least show them that there is an alternative, by involving them in a GEMS activity that reaches the same objectives.

☞ I can coordinate these units into our Teacher's Resource Guide so our teachers will know when to use them.

☞ I am introducing literature based on survival. Do reading to see what the imaginary character would live on if they lived on an island. We are using *Island of the Blue Dolphins*; *My Side of the Mountain*; and *Call of the Wild*. The kids can read it together, plan, and do a talk together.

☞ Important to integrate science with other subjects, since we all have a hard time making science fit—if integrated we can count the time for other subjects too.

☞ In our district we have a calendar to schedule science times. We've gone from no science instruction to good compliance, because we have several staff developers whose job it is to be out in the schools. Follow-up contact on site is important.

☞ In a *Science and Children* article that scared me, it said people who have a mistaken *impression* of a scientific fact or concept will not change their minds just by reading about what the actual fact or concept is, because first impressions are so lasting. Through hands-on learning you can really change those first impressions. Explain this to other teachers to help underline the need for activity-based curricula.

☞ Incorporate use of GEMS with computer programs: simulations would go nicely, for example, one on titration in chemistry or a trip to MARS as in *Oobleck*. **In general, enhance the integration of computer technology in math and science lab work and classes.**

☞ We need a more interdisciplinary approach. Lots of language arts, not just math and science, even in higher levels.

☞ May need to work with textbooks but at least try to get away from **abominable** texts.

☞ Involve the emotions of poetry and literature in science.
(Editor's Note: Please see the GEMS literature handbook, Once Upon A GEMS Guide: Connecting Young People's Literature to Great Explorations in Math and Science.)

Not only gifted and talented students, but also Special Education students can use these activities, since they too can succeed.

☞ Often an activity that teachers like is done every year in a school, so kids get sick of it. It is better to articulate by grade level.
(Editor's Note: On the other hand, doing the same activity over the course of time can provide students with a sense of their progress, and can help bring out the multilayered nature of some activities. For example, a first grader who did Investigating Artifacts, *and who did the activities again in fourth grade would explore in greater depth, and have a great—and far from boring—experience both times! This holds true for most of the activity-based science lessons we know.)*

☞ One of the evaluation items should be safety. Safety gets more important as you go up; so start with early grades, give a grade for safety.

☞ Hands-on science and math activities can be used to good effect in the development of remedial programs, such as those in math, those for high school students, etc.

☞ Plan to fit what you decide rather than what the administrator wants.

☞ Relate to other areas, measurement in math for example, so you are teaching two things at once.

☞ Set up a committee and have tasks delegated using resources, etc. (planning). This way it comes from teachers. This takes work, but is better articulation between grade levels, too.

☞ Be a leader in your district by joining the curriculum committee.

☞ Some of the school districts lock teachers into teaching toward a test; they are afraid to leave something out that they are accountable for. They have a limited number of hours and rigid requirements. Overcome that by changing to different assessments.

☞ Evaluate to see if children have developed scientific thinking skills.

☞ We have laws mandating that students have instructions in different languages. Incorporate your science lesson into this by including a cultural aspect. Research in other cultures, such as the "Ancient Models of the World" activity in *Earth, Moon, and Stars*, brings in other cultures and other languages. Students learn the science faster and better with hands-on approach. We are setting up multicultural centers, with bilingual aspects. These materials are very helpful.
(Editor's Note: GEMS is translating all student data sheets into Spanish.)

☞ Agitate to have activity-based science and mathematics written into the curriculum, included prominently in state and district frameworks and guidelines, etc. so it is required of teachers.

☞ At-risk students: activity-based programs would motivate students, reading is not so much a prerequisite to success, and their success rate will go up.

☞ Cooperative learning: do students complete successfully? are they arguing nicely, etc. give grades on social skills.

☞ For assessment, I have students create a hypothesis and do a procedure and come up with a conclusion; that tells me if they understand the process.

☞ How about a GEMS assessment handbook? *(Editor's Note: We did it! See the GEMS handbook* Insights and Outcomes: Assessments for Great Explorations in Math and Science. *)*

☞ Have a schedule for the school district to rotate kits around schools. This would lay out curriculum for teacher, would allow for consistent teaching and articulate between grade levels. You would know what you would do at your school in what month. Teachers are territorial, and this would also eliminate kids having bubble-ology three times, etc.

☞ Have kids write everything they know about the subject being explored before the day of the activity and then after.

☞ Homework can be a written report of the activity done in class.

☞ One of the most important things that can happen in elementary school is that students want to do more science; allow for extensions that kids may want to do.

☞ If we turn around and start grading them right away it will turn them off. How do we grade on volley ball? We grade on participation! You have to find out a way to do that in your classroom.

☞ If you are going to adopt another textbook, make sure that it is an activity-based program.

☞ If you connect any GEMS unit with district curriculum, no objections possible.

- Invite all first grade teachers to one workshop, so you don't get the repetition. Otherwise the kids get the same M&M activity six years in a row.

- Make up a directory of activities that accompany an existing curriculum.

- Often you can find a connection between GEMS and content areas that you might not have expected. With current emphasis on thematic connections, it is easy to find a connection.

- Organize the science curriculum so grade levels are coordinated. Start with school, then expand to district.

- Show how integration of curriculum can make life easier.

- Show teacher how to integrate different disciplines into their curriculum. For example, have a month on crime lab stuff, relating math and English.

- Tie together science, technology, and society.

- To justify hands-on activities, a particular objective is needed so that principal, parents, and kids know why.

- Units such as *Oobleck* can be integrated into social studies, science and technology and society.

- When we generate numerical data, quantify our results and generate conclusions based on the data, we tie into math lessons.

- Where does science fit in? We're not always the experts. One way is to have a group consensus among students about which science activities are most relevant to them and why—gives them a sense of participation.

- Write to the *GEMS Network News* with your ideas!!

Meet with, Educate, and Gain Support from Your District Administrators

- Discuss activity-based mathematics and science with your school superintendent, or officials in charge of curriculum, so they will support teacher workshops, purchases of activity guides, supplies, and equipment.

- Make a presentation at a School Board meeting. Present hands-on science, or show a video of your students at work. Tell what they can do to support activity-based science, including release time for teachers, staff development, and a budget for supplies and equipment.

- Encourage the appointment of a district science coordinator who can provide workshops, order materials, organize kits, equipment, and curriculum priorities, and in general be an advocate for activity-based math and science in your district.

The school principal is key. Be sure to invite school principals to activity-based science and mathematics workshops along with their teachers. Implementation of more activity-based science works if the principal wants it to work!

- Educate vice-principals and other supervisors to be aware that some activity-based science can be messy and noisy, and still be very educationally effective.

- Supervisors and appraisers of teachers need to emphasize criteria for good teaching such as: Are students engaged in inquiry? Are they asking questions? Are they involved in collecting and analyzing their own data? Are they discussing ideas and drawing conclusions?

☞ Point out the great savings to your district if **you** present workshops rather than hiring teacher-educators from outside the district. Use this as a lever to request release time for the participants and funds for GEMS guides and materials kits.

Offer to present a GEMS activity at a district or principals' meeting. Get the principals interested in the educational advantages of activity-based science, then discuss the importance of administrative support.

☞ To change attitudes in science, there should be workshops for teachers and **principals.**

☞ Communicate a strong commitment to hands-on science and mathematics to the school/district administration and the public.

☞ Convince parents, because they can push the administrators. Have a family hands-on science evening, where the children teach parents in a learning station situation. The parents will change their way of thinking. Invite administrators who will then start to think. It may take a few years, but they will start putting things into place.

☞ For an in-service, we brought in the school board members and even superintendents to do hands-on science.

☞ Consider situations from the administrators' angle: Insist that science gets its fair time in the curriculum. At budget-making time, make sure there is money enough for the kinds of changes we've been talking about.

☞ Get principals involved. Have a principals' workshop, have them do paper towel testing, etc. Get principals and chief administrators to give teachers time off to learn and teach GEMS programs.

☞ Make sure at least one of the principal's class observations is in the activity-based science area.

☞ Have "science clusters" in every elementary school, with free administrative periods rather than lunch duty. Administrators can then spend the prep period assisting the teachers.

☞ Invite school board and administrators (superintendent, principals, etc.) to come and see what you are doing. Have them actually participate in the activities.

☞ Invite upper level administrators to an "Oobleck" workshop, to realize need for sinks and "cornstarch funds."

☞ It is sometimes easier to ask for forgiveness than for permission. And, it is often so successful that you will win over administrators.

☞ Make sure there is enough time allowed in planning for preparation and cleanup. Principals need to know that time is necessary.

☞ Most of us work at schools where they say, this is what you CAN do. In other schools, it's this is what you CANNOT do. This gives us the added responsibility of educating our own administrators, superintendents, and school boards.

☞ Contact the Principals As Leaders in Science (PALS) organization. Are there PALS Leaders in your state?

☞ Supervisors need to know that not every lesson needs to finish at one time, and not every group needs to come up with the same list or answer.

☞ Campaign for and build support from your system-wide administrators. Teachers need to feel that administrators are aware that this kind of science needs to be taught and that the $$$ is there to support it.

- ☞ Make it clear that much of activity-based science is sufficiently open-ended that it requires more than a 45-minute slot, and will be well worth it!

- ☞ Use interested and enthusiastic students for public relations.

- ☞ Very important for principals to set up petty cash funds within schools for teachers—otherwise it can get expensive for teachers.

- ☞ We have to educate school boards, administrators, other teachers and parents. Sometimes school systems change teachers' assignments from year to year so they do not develop a repertoire.

- ☞ Invite administrators to come to the classroom and take part in an entire three-or four-day activity.

- ☞ Use Bloom's taxonomy to show how this kind of hands-on activity encourages higher level thinking.

- ☞ We have a small school and often have to give a report to the people who hold the purse strings. Do this for administrators.

- Do a lot of orientation with administrators. My principal thought that the noise level was too high and I thought the kids were well behaved that day! Administrators must be educated about what to expect.

- ☞ Encourage administrators to attend workshops with you and then help you in the classroom!

- ☞ Get administrators to give teachers time to share, as we are doing now. Actually do it and critique the lesson with other teachers. It is a rare luxury to be able to share!

- ☞ Get administrators to support the idea that science is fun and involving, not difficult and boring.

- ☞ Have administrators cover your class while you go to another teacher's class to model a lesson.

- ☞ You must have a commitment from the administration and the entire staff at the building level; they must have something in their budget; when they work on building improvement plans they must have science incorporated in that plan.

- ☞ Once a month, the principal takes your regular classroom and you do science with all different grades. To set up "Bubble-ology" for the whole school is difficult; so it is best to team-teach or have resource teachers. *(Editor's note: The GEMS guide* Bubble Festival *lends itself to all-school presentation, as do* Mystery Festival *and* Build It! Festival.*)*

- ☞ Organize teachers to propose a different schedule to the administrators so longer time slots are available for doing science activities.

- ☞ To get support, do an activity at a monthly principal's meeting.

- ✍ Write to the *GEMS Network News* with your ideas!!

Classroom Logistics Suggestions, Helpful Hints, and Other Ways to Ease the Shift to Activity-Based Science and Mathematics Teaching

Comments on this subject could be a book in themselves, and many practical aspects are already embodied and embedded in GEMS guides and handbooks.

☞ I like that each GEMS unit is self-contained. You could, for example, still use the textbook, and try just one GEMS unit. Then teachers will be able to use another unit and shift gradually from textbook as source of information, to a whole range of programs of activity-based science. That helps to overcome the initial resistance, and then teachers are sold, because it is more rewarding to teach and easier!

☞ Start small; do one unit at a time.

☞ There is not enough time to prep and clean up—with classes coming in back-to-back it is very difficult. What helped me with cleanup and prep are small trays or shoe boxes. Line up 15 trays with materials in the morning, then later you can distribute them and then pick it back up—whisk it away, and then have the discussion.

☞ Evolve different ways to set up groups so you have heterogenous ability levels.

I work in an inner-city school, and I use hands-on activities as a reward. It works! With a textbook I have a lot more discipline problems.

☞ I would like to see kids more accountable. Make worksheets out after kids have done Oobleck, and in many other ways emphasize accountability and assessment.

☞ Exchanging experiences in this workshop has helped me have more to go on—things like the noise level, fear of not being a science teacher have worried me, but now I feel more reassured. It takes an extra push to do it the first time; amazing how much easier the second time.

☞ Deal with the practicality of how to get this into the classroom. With GEMS, materials lists and simple equipment helps. By having lesson plans all written up, a lot more teachers are more certain of themselves.

☞ Try to provide a relaxed, open-ended, non-pressured environment for children when working on science and mathematics.

☞ If kids are not experienced they may not handle group work with materials well at first. So, start them working in groups in other situations such as spelling. Then they have the expectation of group work already in place. So adding the materials is not such a big step for the kids. The kids will adjust to the transition from small group to whole class.

☞ Setting up classroom learning stations instead of presenting a class unit can help students learn at their own pace, and provide time to do both other units and the learning station hands-on activities.
(Editor's Note: GEMS festival guides feature classroom learning stations.)

☞ Eliminate textbooks by using laser disks/resource books.

☞ Evaluation must be changed from multiple choice.

- ☞ Assessment: Follow-up activities and projects or oral discussions with points for participation.

- ☞ Try to avoid scheduling activity-based lessons at the times of day when students are most frequently pulled out of class for other activities.

- ☞ Classroom management: to provide structure for potentially disruptive kids, prepare carefully, make consistent routines. Give kids leadership tasks.

- ☞ File folders for each student (save one-fourth of the year at a time).

- ☞ For classroom management, have a consistent way of doing things so the kids get used to it, for example, the FOSS program's "getters" and "doers" or the team roles assigned in many GEMS units.

- ☞ For clean-up, assign student for pick-up and clean-up of whole group. Everything must be clean before leaving.

- ☞ Give more responsibility to students for set up and clean up. Have a checklist for students at beginning of lab.

- ☞ Have equal access to all "jobs" in activities.

- ☞ Have extra activities ready for students who finish ahead of time. Provide range of activities for all abilities.

- ☞ Offer to trade cleaning the cafeteria for use of it for certain activities.

- ☞ Have kids help you evaluate the activity (did they like it? did they learn a lot?)

- ☞ Pace well; don't try too much.

- ☞ Prepare all things well including how to wrap up data.

- ☞ Smile! It relieves the anxiety of the kids.

- ☞ Teach hands-on science and mathematics in the morning.

- ☞ Move students to one room for science—only one room gets dirty.

- ☞ Phillips Petroleum sponsors "Search for Solutions" a number of 15-minute videos about fingerprints that could be used in connection with the GEMS activities.

- ☞ The MASK Hotline is a free 800 number at the University of Colorado. You as a teacher can call with any science or math question.

- ☞ Connect GEMS units to other good science/math resources and wider topic areas, for example, the Bank Street Lab has material on convection, *Earth, Moon, and Stars* and *Height-O-Meters* would fit wonderfully into a navigation unit, GEMS guides on mapping fish and animal habitats could be integrated into a larger unit on the environment and ecosystems, the *Magic of Electricity* and *Hot Water Warm Homes*, as part of a study of solar energy, "Water Water Everywhere" with *Discovering Density*, etc.

Write to the *GEMS Network News* with your ideas!!

Gather Support from a Broad Base of Individuals in Your Community

Get the Support of Your Students and Their Parents

☞ Invite your students to display the results of their science and mathematics activities during an open house.

☞ Have your students present a demonstration of hands-on science and mathematics at a PTA (Parent Teachers Association) meeting.

☞ Have parents and teachers at a PTA actually do an activity. Some people have used "Oobleck" for this purpose; others choose a less "messy" activity, such as those in *Fingerprinting* or *Convection*.

☞ Set up a "Bubble-ology" table for parents and teachers at an open-house, or just before a PTA meeting. Have your students standing by to help the parents do activities.

- Make a video of your students in action for showing at a PTA meeting. A video of a rocket launching, as in the GEMS guide *Experimenting with Model Rockets* is very exciting to watch.

- Invite parents who are professionals in various fields to make presentations on their work in your classroom.

- Obtain copies of the *GEMS Parent's Handbook* and hand it out to interested and involved parents.

- Send home a newsletter saying what you are doing in science, and how parents can support your efforts at home by doing additional activities, helping students with home assignments, and sending materials to school.

- Send "Oobleck" home in ziplock bags so the students can show their parents. Other efforts at "guerrilla science" can help to create a "science revolution" at home! (For more bag thickness you could use double bags, or "freezer" ziplock bags.) Send home other activities for parents and students to do together.

- Hold evening or Saturday sessions for families. Present GEMS activities so parents can work with their own children. Later they can continue at home.

- Use the GEMS video to show to teachers or parents.

- Appoint kids to be reporters for a local newspaper.

- Balloon launch day to signal Oobleck in your class.

- Distribute GEMS brochures to a whole school.

- Get parents to go out and buy cornstarch, or make color analyzers for you.

Get kids to write and publish a science activity in the school newspaper.

- Give shows to PTAs so the public gets involved.

- GEMS would make a great parent workshop idea—do with the parents so they can learn to do them with their kids. Hand out the *Parent's Guide to GEMS* and have other books with at-home science/math activities on display. Investigate bringing Family Math and Family Science workshops to your area. *(Editor's Note: The Family Math program is based at the Lawrence Hall of Science. Family Science is based at the Northwest EQUALS program at Portland State University.)*

- Have classes make charts and graphs and post in hall.

- Have displays set up for parent conferences.

- Have a Science Fair, using GEMS and other activities. Demonstrate to parents.

- Have Oobleck at a science fair. Use Oobleck or Bubble-ology to illustrate what a good science project is. Have Oobleck or Bubble-ology set up where people are waiting to get into parent's meeting.

- Have parents do paper towel testing at a PTA meeting.

- Have a science newsletter with at-home projects for parents and older brothers and sisters.

- Have students do a presentation at PTA, so other people can see GEMS activities. Parents love to know something like this is going on.

- ☞ Heart dissection—we found out that a parent was a heart surgeon. He came in and helped show how a heart works! He gave an interesting speech on how computers were part of it. The most important thing is getting the parents involved.

- ☞ Home activity sheet that parent signs give information on what kids are doing.

- ☞ Home-schooling bulletin has a "Science Corner" to spark energy.

- ☞ In my middle school, all students helped landscape our school by planting trees and developing an arboretum on site; and also put up signs of various rock formations so the kids could take field trips right on campus! Kids would come back and ask, 20 years later, "How is my tree doing?"

- ☞ Instead of home room parents, have "science parents" who come with activities.

- ☞ Involve parents in making manipulative materials available. Getting parents used to the move from a "neat" textbook approach to more "messy" hands-on is sometimes not easy.

- ✎ Involve students in writing communications to parents and the public.

- ☞ Kids hear from other kids on playground about experiments—and then they really want to do it!

- ☞ Have students make a science or math video and screen it to parents at home.

- ☞ Once a year we run a "Science Superday" where kids bring their GRANDPARENTS and we do science with them for the day.

Instead of a high-achievement, competitively-oriented science fair (when too often parents build exhibits and students stand back) we decided on a **science festival**. For primary grades, I did half-hour lessons. I had workshops and taught the parents how to do the activities, so they would see what we mean by "process" and understand when we said we did not necessarily want more content, but for the kids to "become scientists," to do what scientists do. We rotated and parents taught the lessons. We did slime, GEMS Crime Lab, and five others. The kids took something they'd made or worked with away with them after each session—the PTA funded it. We had 32 parents teaching it. Teachers went around watching lessons being modeled. Then we had a parent's evening where the parents facilitated, and kids did activities for the public. We had a great turnout; did owl pellets, all sorts of activities. **KIDS SAID IT WAS THE BEST YEAR OF THEIR WHOLE LIVES.**

- ☞ One thing you can do after this workshop is put together a request for $50 or whatever to PTA, so they will know you can do workshops on earthworms or whatever. Groups like PTA really like to hear specifics.

- ☞ Parent curriculum advisory group, can have input into what will be taught.

- ☞ Open-House activities. To increase parental awareness, we bring in kids to do science activities for parents—even have parents blow bubbles in the classrooms. We also have parents supply all of the science equipment, coordinated through open houses.

- ☞ Parents come in: I teach lesson to parents in the morning, the parents stay in the lab and help teach the lesson to small children. Even parents who don't speak English can teach in Spanish or other languages.

- ☞ Post signs asking: "What Is Oobleck?" "What is Bubble-ology?" Then show them two weeks later!

- ☞ Video a classroom actually involved in science activity, then show it at a PTA meeting or to administrators.

- ☞ Video students doing discovery activities, show at Back to School Night.

- ☞ We have a model called "Science Champions"—a group of 5th graders work with kindergarten students. The fifth graders are responsible for presenting appropriate activities, such as loop-the-loops, Bernoulli principle, etc. The idea is not so much that the kindergarten students learn it all but that they are exposed to hands-on science; it piques their curiosity and maybe that will also get their teachers interested. The main idea is to reach the kids and have them get to the teachers. We had 25 students this year, in teams of five. One person is spokesperson, others take part and help. This is a program of the Pacific Science Center. One main topic was whales; salt water was another. The kids have the responsibility to come back and share with the rest of the school. It works!

- ☞ We have nine elementary schools feeding into one junior high. I would like to have the Mathematics Engineering and Science Achievement (MESA) students take the materials into the elementary schools and act as teachers for the elementary students, using these neat GEMS science activities.

- ✎ Write a newsletter to parents with follow-up activities to do at home.

- ☞ Consider a workshop for parents to teach what inquiry science is, have students do the activity.

- ✎ We have a school newspaper, with a science column.

- ✎ Prepare a booklet for parents: "How to Live Through Your Child's Science Project."

- ☞ Create a "science backpack" for students to do activities at home; include instructions and materials.

- ☞ At Back to School night, hand out a questionnaire about parent expertise. Also send the questionnaire home with other materials.

- ☞ Use bulletin boards and other displays to promote science projects.

- ☞ Explain that hands-on science is not only fun, it's important, useful, relevant to real-life. (Sometimes students might not take the class seriously because they see it only as play, and have so much fun.) It's important to let kids know the science and math that is involved in fun activities; good PR for their parents too.

- ☞ Set up a Family Box with motivating activities for students to take home; include an evaluation form.

- ☞ Encourage gifted and talented students to create a hands-on learning center or lesson, then go teach it themselves. They acquire all kinds of skills in addition to science, and teach the science to the little kids.

Have a Family Math or Family Science series. Involving the parents is really a plus.

- ☞ Have an **ungraded** science project (not part of science fair), involves **all** students.

✍ Have kids keep science journals to let their parents know what they did.

Have a GEMS fair, a mini-hands-on science fair; where kids set up for other kids.

☞ Encourage home/school interaction on a particular topic. At the end of a two-week project, invite parents to the classroom for hands-on experience. For example, Earth Day is a good day to build something around.

☞ I've had experiments where the kids do them at home, and parents get even more involved than the students.

☞ In asking for parental involvement, use the Woodrow Wilson quote, "Responsibility is how one builds greatness." Take responsibility for getting something done.

Involve parents, using their areas of expertise; many occupations have key science or math components that are often overlooked, from cooking and baking to accounting, building, water purification, and numerous others.

☞ Primary Science Fun Days; have different activities in different rooms so kids can circulate. Like a Science Olympiad but for lower grade levels.

☞ Start a "classroom exploratorium" with table top exhibits. GEMS festival and exhibit guides are ideal for this.

☞ Translate GEMS and other hands-on materials into Spanish.
(Editor's Note: GEMS is translating all the data sheets into Spanish. We hope additional translations of teacher's guides into Spanish and perhaps other languages will follow.)

✍ Write to the *GEMS Network News* with your ideas!!

Get the Support of Community Leaders and Groups

☞ Take pictures of your students, and send the photos to your local newspaper with a short story about your science classes.

☞ Invite your local newspaper to send a photographer or reporter to your school to do a story on your science program. Contact television and radio reporters too.

☞ Have your students demonstrate science activities in hospital children's wards, or at nursing homes for senior citizens.

✍ Write articles about your school for teachers' magazines, such as *The Instructor*, the *GEMS Network News*, or *Science And Children*. Announcements of such publications can be included in your local newspaper.

☞ Ask for assistance from Lions Club, senior citizens organizations, Elks, etc. These volunteers can help raise money for science supplies, help assemble kits, or assist you in the classroom.

☞ Plan a Saturday Science Day for your entire community, where teachers can attend hands-on workshops, and commercial companies can provide demonstrations and exhibits about their products.

☞ Almost all of us have local museums, including children's museums. Contact people there and design some joint projects.

☞ Science museums can adapt some GEMS or other activities to current exhibits. We are planning to do animal behavior and problem solving activities when the psychology exhibition opens.

- Bring retired teachers who are experienced in hands-on science and math in to teach in-service workshops and model methods.

- Develop a children's science column in the local newspaper; teachers will see an idea and grab onto it.

Plan, publicize and hold a citywide "Oobleck" or "Bubble-ology" day!

- Community college system could provide a central checkout system for GEMS and other hands-on publications along with a lending library for materials.

- Contact Head Start, Girl Scouts, YMCA, as well as many other youth organizations. GEMS activities are perfect for their use.

- Create a Science Club at a college—try out different ideas to draw creativity out of students, then get them started helping out in the schools.

- Delivery system: Some schools in local school districts have local TV channel. Use a participatory approach to presenting GEMS activities on these channels.

- Contact local zoos and botanical gardens—lots of these activities will be helpful there.

- Make sure GEMS and other resources are included on electronic bulletin boards.

- Find out who else is involved in GEMS in your area. It is always nice to do it with someone else. *(Editor's Note: The GEMS National Office can help you get in touch with GEMS Associates or Leaders in your area. And don't forget to contact a GEMS Center or Network Site, if there is one in your region.)*

- Gather and list community resources. Put together a list of possible guest speakers from the community, maybe organized by various science/math units.

- Get together with Park Departments.

- Make a list of contact people who have capabilities in teaching science, or can help other teachers.

- Have a big display featuring hands-on activities at open house. Keep a camera on hand and take a roll of black and white pictures to send to the local paper.

Have non-traditional career role models, for example, a woman as an architect or pilot, male nurse, multicultural role models, etc. All kinds of people can succeed at different jobs—emphasize equality of opportunity. Have these role models show how what is being taught relates to their work, and to the students' lives. One good, accessible way to get this across is to have students play 20 questions to guess what the person does or how she uses math and science.

- Involve community clubs and organizations, conduct a hands-on activity at a meeting, then ask for financial aid.

- It would be nice to have a resource person to bring in information about what workshops and resources are available.

- Monetary commissions for GEMS Leaders. *(Editor's note: Would that it could be so!)*

- Nature stores are becoming very popular. GEMS could be sold at such stores, such as "The Nature Company." In Northampton, for example, we have a store called "A to Z."

- Write postcards to politicians about the need for activity-based science.

- The National Association for the Education of Young Children (NAEYC) has a publication entitled "Developmentally Appropriate Practice for Early Childhood Programs—Serving Children from Birth through Age 8." This is a very good publication that is hands-on in all areas, and is an accumulation of research studies that can be very effective when discussed with administrators.

- One school was just selected as an A+ school by *The Instructor* magazine. Send in an article about your school. Write articles about special efforts you've tried for magazines and journals.

- PBS-TV in my state is planning video workshops with the Education Commissioner. One of these workshops could feature the GEMS activities we did today!

- Pittsburgh Regional Center for Science Teachers is an organization you can call and ask: "I'm doing a unit on animals next week; please send me information." They will send you a printout from the computer of all of the resources they know about, on many different topics and subjects. It is an invaluable resource. Call and get on their mailing list; they have a newsletter. Their database is a two-way street; they like you to give them information too.

- Present activities and information, slide presentations to: Board of Education, Principals, parent groups, School board meetings, Chamber of Commerce, Middle School Club Leaders, church/parish/social service organizations.

- *Science and Children* and *Science* publish articles from schools that use hands-on science in exemplary or novel ways.

- Plan a special project, make sure the media is there—that will help parents get excited.

- Take part in and support programs that are aimed at increasing and equalizing the participation of women and minorities in math and science. In our area we have a special summer program to help prepare less advantaged historically underrepresented students for college.

- Take a copy of the GEMS teacher's guide, put on bulletin board, point out the different guides to people to align with their interests.

- Talk school board members into special activity involving them.

- The Carnegie Museum will lend out study guides.

- We have a science center in the district where teachers come and get credit. We've had a lot of response from elementary teachers that they get a lot of information and build their confidence in science.

- The COMETS Program is very good and focuses on getting women to be involved in science. It is advertised in *Science & Children*.

- The time that we have to fit these activities into all of our subjects is very limited; especially since science is typically on the back burner. We could have outside volunteers, parents, senior citizens, people from industry or business come into the school and help the teacher prepare for the class.

- Use community resources at the local science center, or connected to industry, also constant community resources such as soil testing agencies, weather agencies, etc.

☞ Use GEMS activities in museums to promote visitor interest.

☞ Take advantage of video and satellite communication, as we do in Alaska.

☞ We've encouraged the help of extended families—having grandparents, uncles, or aunts who are not working help. We need to expand and include everyone else, as often both parents are working.

☞ We pulled an experienced hands-on science teacher out of retirement—he used to do a lot of fun things, and we had him come along on a field trip that he used to do, to nearby fossil beds. He loved doing it again, just like a kid in a candy shop. We studied mineral formations, camped out at a lake, did astronomy and river activities, went to caves, observed beaver dams, ended up at a dam and got a tour, etc. Why is it that when people retire, all that great wealth is gone? They often will volunteer their time to help us get our science programs going.

☞ Increase business and industrial collaboration so they can bounce off subjects we're presenting to make connections to careers and demonstrate strong ties between science/math and the real world.

✍ Write articles to the newspaper about what **science educators** are doing.

☞ Colorado Alliance For Science is a group of business people, higher education people, K–12 teachers, etc., trying to improve science education. We try to coordinate resources to let teachers know what is available, to get speakers, judges for science fairs, etc. We also do a lot of visiting with industry.

✍ Computer bulletin board; with local nodes so that people need not make long distance phone calls.

☞ Contact division of wildlife/forest service or state parks to use as a resource. Try the health department or OSHA.

☞ Create a list of science/math resource specialists in your area. Districtwide science directory for experts in different subjects. If you had a question about the Solar System, who would you call?

☞ Displays at local malls.

☞ Guest speakers from business, museums, etc.

☞ Have a demonstration for interested corporate people with photo opportunities.

☞ Have a resident scientist for a week who can do some neat things. Have local naturalists, meteorologists come out to schools.

☞ Have an "expo" throughout the district. Set up tables in the gym and have kids demonstrate on in-service days. See it in action, rather than just see the products. HAVE KIDS TEACH TEACHERS!

☞ In large urban systems around the country, businesses and churches are adopting schools. NASA is adopting a math-science magnet school.

Invite the custodian to lessons. We need the support of the custodian!

✍ It's a common phenomenon that there are lots of resources, but people don't know what they are. Communicate through newsletters.

☞ National Science and Technology Week had a theme of Global Change. They had two packets (developed by BSCS). Check out their yearly packets.

☞ Not just materials, but also resources for information, technology, and expertise can come from industry.

☞ Physics students could create an activity to present to elementary kids. They'd make good role models.

☞ Present to school board, to persuade them of the value of the activities and the need for funding. Make school board members suspects in a make-believe crime in the "Crime Lab Chemistry" activity.

☞ Some teachers don't like to do hands-on with the whole class, so I have one high school student per five students to help the teacher. We call that "mutually-aided learning." The high school teacher teaches the high school students what to do. It is a credit class; they go to the elementary classrooms during the day.

☞ Teachers need to learn how to toot their own horn so that others can know that you are doing really neat things in your classroom.

☞ Team up schools so all benefit from shared support and public relations.

☞ Use your local cable TV for a snapshot of what is happening in the schools.

☞ Videotape or photograph your class in activities and put on bulletin board or show at a meeting.

☞ We contacted local laborers to see how they need science and math in their work. They loved it because they never get to be asked to come to the classroom to talk about their work, and explain in practical terms the real-life connections to math and science. Plumbers, electricians, carpenters, machinists . . .

☞ We had an Air Force instructor come and do a lesson on lenses. He showed us circulation through a fish's tail with a microscope.

We have a group called the "**Aha! Club**," which is what you say when you finally understand something. Our club did a show with neat science demonstrations, sort of a takeoff on Mr. Wizard. The students collected questions from kids, gathered materials from the neighborhood, and videotaped it.

✎ Write to the *GEMS Network News* with your ideas!!

Funding Ideas

Even though the main topics of the discussions at GEMS workshops were exemplary teaching and educational leadership, rather than funding, here are a few good funding ideas.

☞ Periodically, the GEMS project has been able to offer "guide grants" that will provide free GEMS guides for use in workshops and other presentations. The guide grants are announced in the *GEMS Network News*.

☞ The *GEMS Centers Handbook* will include background information on GEMS that may be helpful in grant proposals and in setting up a GEMS Center in your region.

✎ Seek money for science workshops from local universities. Write a grant proposal to get a college to help you teach hands-on science; to a Foundation for a specialized series of presentations on the environment or to educate teachers; as part of a partnership with business or industry.

☞ Persuade administrators of the crucial importance of providing funding, space and a suitable environment to foster activity-based science and mathematics, so they in turn seek adequate funding. Get support from administrators to send colleagues to in-services.

☞ The more you know about the exact purposes and stipulations regarding various funds, such as how they are coded, the better you can design your workshop with all the right code words on it.

✎ Consider writing special proposals to provide activity-based science and mathematics outreach and teacher in-services to "science-poor" students and teachers, to historically underrepresented groups, or other less advantaged populations/neighborhoods.

☞ Seek funds to obtain software.

✎ Get $$$ from grant writing and corporate funds. Teach people how to write grant proposals.

☞ Use the Elementary and Secondary Act monies, Title II funds, Chapter II funds.

☞ Seek grants to help fund minimum days.

☞ Seek PTA contributions, community donations, hold bake sales.

☞ Contact your district and ask about Eisenhower Title II funding, for in-services. It is available for in-service education! Often, if you go to the administrator and offer to write the proposal, then you determine where the funds go. Your district is entitled to those funds; if they do not write the proposal, your district does not get the funds!

☞ Eisenhower Higher Education funds controlled by state agencies are available for college level courses/workshops.

☞ Environmental Education grants from the Department of Education Math-Science Unit can be obtained ($1,000, $3,000, $5,000).

☞ Use School Improvement Project funds.

☞ Seek funds to establish a mentor program—a good way to share with other people in the school or the district. That gives you a budget and more time.

☞ See who is in charge of curriculum in your district; who may be willing to buy guides and allow you to provide workshops.

✎ Write a grant proposal so we can get out and team-teach with people who are less confident, with funds for our release time so we can be resource teachers.

☞ From Eisenhower funds, in the Little Rock school district, we have an in-service training period from 4:00–7:00 p.m., where teachers accumulate hours. There is no cost to teachers for up to 45 hours of in-service; they also get kits of materials to take back to their classrooms. This program was written up in *Science and Children*.

☞ Apply for grants for supplies, e.g. NSTA, License Plate Grant (California), local corporate/business assistance.

☞ Contact local businesses to contribute supplies and equipment to your science classroom, or to the district science resource center. Give them credit in the local newspaper, so other businesses will donate as well.

☞ In California, Pacific Gas & Electric (PG&E) has a grant fund.

☞ Have a local company "adopt a school." They can provide funds, supplies and equipment, volunteers to prepare materials and assist in the classroom, and possibly also bring experts on various subjects to address your students.

- Ask for business/corporate contributions of funds to purchase specialized science and mathematics supplies and equipment.

- Write to the *GEMS Network News* with your ideas!!

Do Activity-Based Science and Math Outside the Classroom

- Invite your students to do mathematics and science activities at recess, lunch time, or after school. Set up learning stations around the school, so kids could do *Build It! Festival* or *Bubble Festival* at recess. Or have a special open period when different activities are offered.

- Establish a science club where students meet to do activity-based science activities. Use GEMS and other activities at science clubs meetings—have students plan ways to present activities in their classes.

- Present after school and summer science and mathematics "Unschool" programs at school sites or Science Centers (after school and on Saturdays).

- Do workshops for providers of children's day-care in how to present science activities.

- Present workshops in GEMS or other science and mathematics activities for leaders of 4-H Clubs, Boy Scouts, Girl Scouts, Cub Scouts, Brownies, Campfire, Inc., YMCAs and summer camps.

- Contact your local parks association regarding opportunities to teach classes, hold star observing parties, or to bring your students on field trips.

- Publish ideas from the GEMS guides in a local newspaper column, explaining how families can do science activities at home.

- Hold an overnight science/mathematics camp-in at a science museum, where students bring sleeping bags and do science and mathematics activities as long as they can stay up.

- Use GEMS activities at birthday parties, festivals, and fairs.

- Plan field trips related to GEMS activities. For example, visit your local police station when doing *Fingerprinting* or *Crime Lab Chemistry*. Visit a pet shop when doing *Animals In Action*. Visit a beekeeper when your students are doing *Buzzing a Hive* activities.

- Plan mini-field trips around the school yard, for example, to gather moon observations in *Earth, Moon, and Stars*, or to collect specimens for *Earthworms*, or to measure the height of the flagpole in *Height-O-Meters*.

- Have science kits in the library for kids to check out and bring home to do follow-up activities.

- At science fair, have students come and do experiments similar to science night.

- Have a science-math club by special invitation, using gender-equitable activities. By special invitation means that kids will be more willing to be there.

- Develop science toys based on science and mathematics principles.

☞ Expand to have districtwide or even statewide programs to compare paper towel brands from different part of the country.

☞ GEMS has good activities for staging a Science Circus.

☞ Have field trip of 1st and 6th graders to go to high school and see chemistry experiments in action.

☞ Have students demonstrate and explain GEMS activities in a children's hospital or for elderly people in a nursing home.

☞ Museum: build activities into exhibits.

Use GEMS activities in after school daycare programs.

☞ Informal "sciencing." Have a room to the side so teachers and kids can do GEMS activities during an Olympiad or other gathering.

☞ Public awareness, present to different clubs, businesses, show what you're doing to get science materials and equipment, and corn starch.

☞ Rocketry or Animal Defenses could be done in different areas, send results to one place for analysis and dissemination to all participating schools. Send in fingerprint data and have national data bank. Personalized pen-pals with fingerprints.

☞ School Museum—teachers and their classes set up displays or discovery rooms that are hands-on, activity-oriented. Other teachers can bring their classes to experience the "classroom museum." GEMS festival and exhibit guides, and the San Francisco Exploratorium's Snackbook, are useful in this connection.

☞ Science leadership camps where students go to camp—peer teaching, etc.

☞ GEMS can be used like the OBIS program has been, in non-traditional situations such as school science clubs, 4-H, Girl Scouts, Boy Scouts, community centers, etc.

☞ Have a week on a neat topic, such as bubble week, and invite every class to participate. Use faculty peer pressure to get everyone involved.

☞ Use GEMS as part of a "Scientist of the Week" program activities from which kids could choose.

☞ Use at environmental education center—family groups who walk in on weekends.

☞ Use with alternative programs for high-risk students.

☞ Use in a peer teaming situations, where fifth graders work with second graders—do activities they can't manage on their own, older kids learn in the process.

Use GEMS activities to train docents who do programs for the public at museums, zoos, and aquariums.

☞ We started lunchroom labs last year in the cafeteria outside—we'd have our classes there, and other teachers would walk in "cold" right there with their kids. Main thing is—don't tell the kids anything. If they ask a question, turn it around and ask, "What do you think?"

☞ Plan activities for last week or days of school that are very involving; like mouse traps, egg drops, etc., getting all of the science classes involved. Do it in a visible area, such as a science activities fair or festival, so all students are involved in it.

☛ Plan a whole day for the whole school: small groups, break time, entirely new experiments never tried before.

☛ Science clubs, summer school classes, and students who may be having learning difficulties can do cooperative, hands-on lessons like these, because they are at no disadvantage if they are not all at the same reading level or if they are not great readers.

☛ Use GEMS activities for summer school enrichment; move away from remedial to enrichment model of summer school.

☛ Use an Olympiad format. Use hands-on science as a motivator, but with cooperative groups, working on group science projects, with ribbons for winning groups.

☛ Teacher supply stores, biological displays, catalogs, bulletin boards, teacher's rooms, cablevision science program, resource libraries, school libraries, sandwich boards, kids at bus stops, parents at airports! skywriting, public domain network, Donahue, Oprah!

✎ Write to the *GEMS Network News* with your ideas!

Acronym Key

AAPT
American Association of Physics Teachers

ACS
American Chemical Society

AIMS
Activities in Math and Science

BSCS
The Biological Sciences Curriculum Study

CEPUP
Chemical Education for Public Understanding Project

COMETS
Career-Oriented Modules for Elementary Teaching of Science

FOSS
Full Option Science System

GEMS
Great Explorations in Math and Science

LHS
Lawrence Hall of Science

MESA
Mathematics, Engineering, and Science Achievement

NAEYC
National Association for the Education of Young Children

NASA
National Aeronautics and Space Agency

NEA
National Education Association

NSF
National Science Foundation

NSRC
National Science Resource Center

NSTA
National Science Teacher's Association

OBIS
Outdoor Biology Instructional Strategies

PTA/PTO
Parent Teacher's Association/Organization

SEPUP
Science Education for Public Understanding Project

TERC
Technology Education Resource Center

Summing Up

We are all aware of the tremendous need for improved science and mathematics education nationwide. This handbook contains information on the educational effectiveness of the GEMS series and the innovative ideas gathered from many thousands of GEMS workshop participants. Changes in the classroom depend ultimately on teachers. Hopefully, GEMS and other activity-based science and mathematics programs will provide much needed assistance to you and other GEMS Associates and Leaders in helping those changes take place.

We very much need, welcome, and appreciate your comments, criticisms, input, letters to the editor of the *GEMS Network News*, new ideas, and concerns. As ideas occur to you for improvements in any GEMS materials, please share them with us. Be an active participant in the ever-changing process that is GEMS.

THANK YOU!

GEMS
Lawrence Hall of Science
University of California
Berkeley, CA 94720
(510) 642-7771

email: gems@uclink4.berkeley.edu

website: lawrencehallofscience.org/gems

LHS GEMS

Great Exporations in Math and Science (GEMS)
Lawrence Hall of Science
University of California
Berkeley, CA 94720
(510) 642-7771 • FAX: (510) 643-0309

Leadership & Workshop Support

GEMS offers a variety of workshop support materials for GEMS Leaders and Associates. Some items are free, while other items require a (refundable) deposit. Shipping costs for borrowed materials are the responsibility of GEMS Leaders, and all **borrowed materials must be returned to the GEMS office no later than one week following the workshop.** There are a limited number of these sets, so please be prompt in returning them. We regret there may be times when requests cannot be filled. To order any GEMS support materials, please complete are return this form to GEMS at least three weeks prior to the date you'd like the materials to arrive. Please complete the **entire** form, and read the instructions in each section carefully. Thank you.

WORKSHOP INFORMATION:

Workshop title _____

Workshop date:_____ Date borrowed materials to be returned _____

Name: _____ Phone: _____

Address: _____

FREE ITEMS: YES, please send me the following free items for workshop participants.

_____ copies of the GEMS Catalog   _____ copies of the
                                                GEMS Network Newsletter

_____ a list of GEMS Associates in my area

ITEMS REQUIRING A DEPOSIT: Make deposit check or puchase order payable to UC Regents, or provide credit card information:

Credit Card # _____ exp. date_____
(VISA, MC, Discover)
Signature_____

YES, I would like to borrow the following Item(s) requiring a deposit:

____ 1 GEMS Introductory Video (8 minutes) $16

____ 1"Threads" Video on GEMS Educational Goals & Objectives (11 minutes) $16

____ 1 set, GEMS Teachers Guides .... (Call for price)

____ 1 set, GEMS Teachers & Assembly Guides .... (Call for price)

____ 1 set, GEMS Teachers Assembly & Exhibit Guide .... (Call for price)

SHIPPING: GEMS will pay shipping costs but you are responsible for return shipping cost. (Please insure)

PURCHASE: These materials are also available for purchase. Please call for prices. We can process your payment if you decide to purchase any materials.

To strengthen the growing ranks of GEMS Leaders nationwide, the GEMS Project has created a new leadership category: the GEMS Associate.

To become a GEMS Associate you must (1) be interested in being an active provider of GEMS workshops to teachers in your region, and (2) complete a GEMS Associate's Workshop, taught by GEMS and Lawrence Hall of Science staff.

Associate's Workshops, which last at least several days, began in 1994 at the Lawrence Hall of Science and may also be held at selected GEMS Centers or Network Sites nationwide, with the direct participation of LHS GEMS staff. While these specialized workshops always include hands-on GEMS activities, they place major emphasis on leadership and workshop presentation strategies, and provide the basis for in-depth familiarity with the approach and philosophy of the GEMS series.

GEMS has now launched intensive three-day Associates II Workshops—highly collaborative and interactive seminars on cutting-edge educational issues. Associates II gatherings are open **only** to those who are already GEMS Associates. Associates II Workshops are held on an annual basis at Lawrence Hall of Science, usually in January. Check the *GEMS Network News* or the GEMS website at *lawrencehallofscience.org/gems* for more information.

To participate in a GEMS Associate's Workshop please contact the GEMS Project at **(510) 642-7771.**

Interested in Becoming a GEMS Associate?

Great Exporations in Math and Science (GEMS)
Lawrence Hall of Science
University of California
Berkeley, CA 94720
(510) 642-7771 • FAX: (510) 643-0309

Leadership & Workshop Support

GEMS offers a variety of workshop support materials for GEMS Leaders and Associates. Some items are free, while other items require a (refundable) deposit. Shipping costs for borrowed materials are the responsibility of GEMS Leaders, and all **borrowed materials must be returned to the GEMS office no later than one week following the workshop.** There are a limited number of these sets, so please be prompt in returning them. We regret there may be times when requests cannot be filled. To order any GEMS support materials, please complete are return this form to GEMS at least three weeks prior to the date you'd like the materials to arrive. Please complete the **entire** form, and read the instructions in each section carefully. Thank you.

WORKSHOP INFORMATION:

Workshop title _____

Workshop date:_____ Date borrowed materials to be returned _____

Name: _____ Phone: _____

Address: _____

_____

FREE ITEMS: YES, please send me the following free items for workshop participants:

_____ copies of the GEMS Catalog   _____ copies of the GEMS Network Newsletter

_____ a list of GEMS Associates in my area

ITEMS REQUIRING A DEPOSIT: Make deposit check or puchase order payable to UC Regents, or provide credit card information:

Credit Card #_____ exp. date_____
(VISA, MC, Discover)
Signature_____

YES, I would like to borrow the following Item(s) requiring a deposit:

____ 1 GEMS Introductory Video (8 minutes) $16

____ 1"Threads" Video on GEMS Educational Goals & Objectives (11 minutes) $16

____ 1 set, GEMS Teachers Guides .... (Call for price)

____ 1 set, GEMS Teachers & Assembly Guides .... (Call for price)

____ 1 set, GEMS Teachers Assembly & Exhibit Guide .... (Call for price)

SHIPPING: GEMS will pay shipping costs but you are responsible for return shipping cost. (Please insure)

PURCHASE: These materials are also available for purchase. Please call for prices. We can process your payment if you decide to purchase any materials.